START & RUN A
BOOKKEEPING BUSINESS

START & RUN A
BOOKKEEPING BUSINESS

Angie Mohr, CA, CMA

Self-Counsel Press
(a division of)
International Self-Counsel Press Ltd.
USA   Canada

Self-Counsel Press acknowledges the financial support of the Government of Canada through the Book Publishing Industry Development Program (BPIDP) for our publishing activities.

Printed in Canada.

First edition: 2006

Library and Archives Canada Cataloguing in Publication

Mohr, Angie
    Start and run a bookkeeping business / by Angie Mohr.

(Self-counsel business series)
ISBN 1-55180-641-X

    1. Bookkeeping. 2. Small business—Management.
3. New business enterprises—Management. I. Title. II. Series.

HF5628.M63 2005   657'.2   C2005-905648-7

Self-Counsel Press
(a division of)
International Self-Counsel Press Ltd.

1704 North State Street	1481 Charlotte Road
Bellingham, WA 98225	North Vancouver, BC V7J 1H1
USA	Canada

CONTENTS

NOTICE TO READERS

Laws are constantly changing. Every effort is made to keep this publication as current as possible. However, the author, the publisher, and the vendor of this book make no representations or warranties regarding the outcome or the use to which the information in this book is put and are not assuming any liability for any claims, losses, or damages arising out of the use of this book. The reader should not rely on the author or the publisher of this book for any professional advice. Please be sure that you have the most recent edition.

ACKNOWLEDGMENTS

Thanks go to many people for their assistance, guidance, and moral support while I wrote this book, including the following:

- ✍ April Bartlett, one of the finest bookkeepers I know and a Mohr & Company alumna

- ✍ The rest of the Mohr & Company gang: Tim Bartlett, Lindsay Mund, Yesenia Torres, Dawn Mantle, Doug Lester, and Karl McAlonen

- ✍ My mom, Judy, who taught me how to be an entrepreneur

- ✍ Everyone at Self-Counsel Press, and especially Richard Day and Aaron Morris

- ✍ Sam Hiyate, the coolest agent anyone could wish for

- ✍ All of my bookkeeping clients over the years, who taught me that there is nothing as important as personal attention

✍ The business leaders and entrepreneurs who have inspired me over the years (sometimes unknowingly), including Karen Maidment, Kim White, Dave Chilton, Tricia Siemens and Chuck Erion, Breen Bentley, the Adlys family, and Lee Brubacher and Chris McNabb

✍ My friends who have put up with prolonged silences and manic e-mails over the past two years: Ali, Jennifer, Rick, Kate, Kim, Rosalynn, Colleen, and Michael

✍ And, as always, last but most importantly, my husband, Jeff, and munchkins Alex and Erika

INTRODUCTION

To those with a "head for numbers" and some computer knowledge, it may seem like a natural thing to put out your shingle and offer bookkeeping services to small businesses and individuals who need to track their investment portfolios.

However, knowing how to keep the books doesn't necessarily translate into business savvy, and many would-be bookkeeping services suffer from the same entrepreneurial ailments as businesses in every other industry. Ninety-six percent of all small businesses in North America that are started today won't be around in ten years, and bookkeeping businesses are no exception. They either go bankrupt, close their doors, or otherwise give up the dream of "making it." Not having a full complement of business management skills leaves business owners in the air without a flight plan.

That's the bad news. The good news is that financial management skills can be learned. These skills include the following:

✍ Human resource management

- Record keeping

- Financial statement analysis

- Budgeting and forecasting

- Billable-time management

Every single entrepreneur who starts a small business can develop and hone business prowess. The added benefit to those who run bookkeeping businesses is that they can pass on these learned skills to their clients, thereby increasing client loyalty and, as a result, fee income.

Accurate record keeping is one of the cornerstones of small-business success. Yet a shocking number of entrepreneurs do not possess this skill. There are over 24 million small businesses in the United States and Canada alone, each with a need to track their business results so that they can interpret the "story" those results are telling them. The process is much like a physician reading lab results (which look like hieroglyphics to the average person) to diagnose what's wrong with a patient. There is a constant need for bookkeepers to help keep businesses both on track with government and taxation reporting and regulations and up to speed with prudent internal reporting requirements. A high-quality bookkeeping business can help its clients track the numbers *and* understand what they mean.

This book is designed for people who want to start or improve their bookkeeping services business. It covers not only the basics of running an entrepreneurial enterprise but also those issues specific to a bookkeeping operation, such as tracking client work, increasing your customer base, and determining when to involve a professional accountant.

There's no need to read this book in the order it has been presented. Feel free to jump in wherever you'd like. Different chapters will naturally appeal to you at different stages of your business start-up. This book will cover such diverse topics as finding the money for your business, pricing your services, working from home, and marketing and promotion.

I do recommend that you eventually read the entire book, for it sheds new light on many critical business subjects and may help you with challenges you didn't even know you had.

One final word about currency. Throughout this book, I use dollars and cents for consistency and ease of use. However, the business principles contained here are equally applicable regardless of the country in which you conduct business and are not directly related to any particular set of accounting rules or tax laws. Terminology may differ from country to country, and the dollar signs for some readers might be pounds or rupees or euros, but the underlying business principles are the same.

As you read the book, drop by our website, <www.numbers101.com> to access our library of business articles, cool biz tools, and other great links and resources for your business. You can also sign up for our monthly e-newsletter while you're there.

For now, please put your luggage in the overhead bins, put your tray tables in the upright position, and prepare for takeoff!

Chapter 1

GETTING STARTED

Before you jump in with both feet, it's useful to take some time to examine your motivation for starting your own business. This will most likely save you vast amounts of time, money, and grief in the future.

Assess Your Skills and Goals

Every business owner/manager has to learn three major skills: building a business, managing a business, and doing what the business does. You may be interested in doing only one of these three things. For example, you might get great pleasure out of hairstyling, but have little patience for managing the day-to-day operations of such a business. In that case, you might want to reconsider your decision to open a hair salon. No matter how much joy it gives you to "be your own boss" while doing the thing you do best, you will come to despise all the other tasks that go along with owning and managing a small business.

On the other hand, you may love building the business: designing the office space, putting together the marketing plan, forecasting, and building the customer base. You may, however, be thoroughly bored with the management aspect or with doing what the business does. Entrepreneurs who feel this way tend to build a business, get it up and running, sell it, and start all over again. The thrill for them is in the creation process.

If you plan to build your business, manage it, and be its chief employee, make sure you have the energy and the skills to do all three things. If not, you will have to hire other people to do the things you do not wish to do yourself — or rethink your business plan entirely.

Worksheet 1 provides some skill-testing questions you should ask yourself as you consider your decision to start a bookkeeping business. If you answer no to any question, you should think about how you will develop skills and knowledge in that particular area, as each is critical to your success as a business owner and manager.

Once you have assessed your strengths and weaknesses in terms of building, managing, and operating a business, it's time to look at your personal goals. Why do you want to start your own business? You may want to start your own business to make more money than you could if you were an employee. You may get a rush from building something from nothing. There are a myriad reasons why entrepreneurs start businesses. Let's look at three of the main motivators: money, freedom, and "empire building."

(a) *Money.* Owning and running a business has the potential for providing you with a higher level of investment return and remuneration than you would receive working for someone else. The profit potential is definitely there, but high profits are a trade-off for high risks. Starting a small business is a risky proposition and you, as the owner, face the potential for financial loss as well as gain. It's important to keep this in mind as you build your business. Make sure you not only have the financial ability to survive failure, but also the ability to tolerate risk.

When small-business owners talk about money, though, they don't usually mean they want money for money's sake. Money means something slightly different to each person, but in general, it represents financial independence, prosperity,

WORKSHEET 1
SKILLS ASSESSMENT

Do you have the skills you need to start a bookkeeping business?		Yes	No
1.	Are you comfortable promoting yourself and your business to prospective clients?		
2.	Do you have experience or training in basic double-entry bookkeeping, up to preparation of financial statements?		
3.	Are you proficient in managing your own schedule?		
4.	Do you know how to analyze your industry and your competitors?		
5.	Do you know how to develop a marketing and promotion strategy for your proposed business?		
6.	Can you manage multiple client engagements at the same time?		
7.	Do you have access to enough financial resources to start your business?		
8.	Do you know how to project your revenues and expenses in the start-up period?		
9.	Can you handle drawbacks and failures?		
10.	Do you have strong "people skills" to deal with clients, suppliers, and employees in an effective way?		
11.	Are the people around you (spouse, children, parents) supportive of your entrepreneurial ambitions?		
12.	Are you willing to spend the time it takes to get a new business off the ground?		
13.	Do you have enough attention to detail to make certain that your business is on track with its financial projections?		

and security. Think about what money represents to you. The more time you spend planning your business model before you begin, the more likely you will be building a profitable enterprise that will meet your personal financial goals.

(b) *Freedom.* Many small-business owners like the freedom that comes with not having a boss and being able to make their own decisions. However, with this freedom comes ultimate responsibility for the business, including responsibility for customer satisfaction, working conditions, supplier short-ages, product failure, and the economic well-being of your employees. Look at whether you are the type of person who can handle these responsibilities while simultaneously making considered, but quick, decisions on a daily basis.

(c) *"Empire building."* For many small-business owners, the most important consideration is that they are building something that will outlive them and perhaps provide income and stability to future generations. If this is an important consideration for you, it will be critical to make sure that you are building a business that has value, and that the value can be transferred to others through sale of the business or inheritance. The unfortunate reality is that over 80 percent of small businesses do not survive into the next generation but die with their owners. Planning ahead for the eventual transfer of ownership will help preserve the value of your business.

Why Bookkeeping?

Now that you've examined your skills and your motivations for becoming an entrepreneur, it's time to assess why you have chosen bookkeeping services as your business's main offering. Here are some questions to ask yourself:

- ✍ Do you currently work as an employee bookkeeper and enjoy the work?

- ✍ Do you feel there is an unmet market need for bookkeeping services?

- ✍ Do you think you can fill a certain niche and attract business because of your different way of doing things?

Take some time to write down your rationale for starting a book-keeping services business as if you had to explain it to a group of people. The better you can articulate your reasoning, the more it will solidify and reinforce your focus and commitment. You will need to do this exercise as part of your business plan (discussed later in this chapter).

Approaches to Starting Your Business

Once you have definitively decided that you want to start a bookkeeping services business, there are two ways you can go about it. You can build your practice from scratch, customer by customer, or you can buy an existing practice. There are benefits and downsides to both approaches. You will have to assess which considerations are most important to you and your situation. Let's look at these considerations.

Building a business from scratch

When you build a business from scratch, you will start with nothing but the tiniest grain of an idea. You will spend months or longer mapping out that idea, running cash-flow scenarios, doing market and competitive analysis, writing a business plan and a management operating plan, and working on the business's vision and mission statements. You will be meeting with bankers, accountants, lawyers, and financial planners as you build your external advisory team.

You will probably open your doors before you take in the first dollar in revenue, and you will take the enormous leap of faith that customers will actually want the services you are selling as you had envisioned in your business plan.

The process may sound scary, but designing and building the business that exists in your head can be an extremely fulfilling and gratifying experience — so much so that many successful entrepreneurs design and build businesses, then sell them once they're up and running. Then they start all over again and build another one.

Here are the pros of building a business from scratch:

- ✍ You can design internal systems the way you want them to work right from the beginning
- ✍ It can be less expensive than buying an existing operation
- ✍ There is no risk of acquiring the previous owner's liabilities or having to satisfy pre-existing warranties

Designing and building the business that exists in your head can be an extremely fulfilling and gratifying experience.

✍ You can manage staffing needs more carefully (i.e., you don't inherit employees that are sub-par and/or difficult to fire)

There are also some cons to building a business from scratch:

✍ Attracting investors can be more difficult and expensive. Because the venture doesn't yet exist, investing will be a riskier proposition.

✍ Generating profits can take longer than with an existing business

✍ Building name recognition and goodwill with customers can take a long time

✍ There is a much greater risk of failure than with a business that has a proven track record

Buying an existing business

Buying an existing business is, in general, less of a risk for you as the major investor. You have the opportunity to watch the business in action, and you will be able to access the historical financial information to determine patterns such as growth rate, profitability, and solvency. You know that you will be able to generate a return on your investment almost immediately as well as be remunerated for your management role in the business (and perhaps also your operational role).

You may choose to buy a business because you want to quickly introduce a new product to an existing customer base before there are too many competitors in the market. For example, if you have developed a brand-new print-on-demand self-serve book station, you may want to have instant access to a thriving bookstore's customers before copycats come on the market.

Here are some of the pros of buying an existing business:

✍ Obtaining external financing can be easier than if you build a business from scratch because the business has a track record

✍ You can market your existing products to a new customer base

✍ Managing and fine-tuning an existing business model can be easier than building it from the ground up

✍ You can generate profits right from the purchase date

✍ You can continue the business with the existing goodwill and name recognition

The cons to buying an existing business include the following:

✍ You may be inheriting the hidden headaches of the previous owner

✍ You may be inheriting negative goodwill if the business has a bad name in the community

✍ It may take as long to reshape the business the way you want it as it would have taken had you started a new business from scratch

✍ The clients you are "buying" may have only been loyal to the former owner and may choose not to stay on as clients when you take over

Decide which priorities are most important to you and make your decision to build or buy a business based on sound reasoning.

Setting Up Your Own Books

There are many different ways you can set up the books for your bookkeeping practice. You may not have given this much thought, because primarily you help others with *their* bookkeeping. However, as a bookkeeping practice, you will need to keep the following goals and objectives in mind when considering what type of system to use:

✍ *You will need to track your time spent on each client.* Even if you don't do your billings based on time spent (more on this in chapter 3), you will still need to assess what your recovery rate is so that you can understand your efficiency. The system you choose should be able to track time by client in a clear, concise way.

✍ *You will need to track separately the revenues from each of the services you offer.* When you analyze your financial statements, you will need to know which of your areas of practice (such as monthly business bookkeeping, taxes, and investment tracking) are growing and which are the most profitable.

✍ *You will need a system that can be updated quickly and easily.* You don't want your own set of books to be onerous and take up time that could be spent on client work.

There is always a balance in any business enterprise between time and money.

Choosing Your Accounting Software

Given these general system requirements, what accounting software should you choose? And how will you know when it's time to upgrade? Your considerations when choosing your first system are the same as when you will upgrade in the future. If you keep in mind your potential future record-keeping needs, this will help with your initial decisions.

You will at some point outgrow your current accounting system, whether you started out with a manual ledger, an Excel or Lotus spreadsheet, or simply a shoe box (or refrigerator box, depending on the number of receipts your business accumulates).

The need for a new accounting system may manifest itself in many different forms. You may find that payroll is becoming more onerous to calculate and track as you hire more employees. A manufacturing or resale business may keep running out of stock on high-turnover items because they are out before they know it. In a service business, you may start losing track of how much time should be billed to each customer. Regardless of the various symptoms, the problem remains the same: your bookkeeping system is taking more of your time than it's worth.

There is always a balance in any business enterprise between time and money. You can spend either time or money (or both). Scrimping on one will cost you more of the other. For example, if you decide to buy the least-frills accounting package you can find on the shelves of your local office supply store, you may spend an extra ten hours per week forcing it to do what you want it to do. If you could take that ten hours and use it to sell more to your customers, then perhaps it would be worth spending more on the software package.

Recently, Deloitte & Touche did a study of the top criteria used by businesses when selecting their bookkeeping software. It's quite interesting to see that first-time business owners and seasoned entrepreneurs have different priorities in this regard. This would suggest that experience teaches business owners what's really important when choosing financial software.

The top three criteria used by first-time business owners when selecting bookkeeping software are —

(1) price of software,

(2) ease of implementation, and

(3) ease of use.

These reasons make sense. They are all important things to consider in the purchasing decision. But now take a look at the top three criteria used by businesses selecting their second bookkeeping system —

(1) level of support provided by the local firm

(2) developer's track record of performance

(3) software's ability to fit the business

What do the experienced business owners know that the neophytes don't? Let's take a look at each point separately.

Level of support provided by the local firm

Many of the entry-level accounting systems are billed as being turn-key systems; you just load the software and you're up and running. However, setting them up is never quite that simple. It's important to make sure that you can easily and economically access customer and technical support for your new system. Some software companies charge for support calls, which is fine as long as you can get hold of someone when you need them. You will also want to consider whether there are consultants based locally that can come into your business and provide customized setup and training. When you're looking at consumer reviews of the product, pay special attention to what they say about support.

Developer's track record of performance

A first-time software buyer may very well discount the importance of how well the software has worked in the past, but seasoned entrepreneurs understand how much time it takes to work around bugs in the software or to install patches to fix problems as they arise. Keep in mind that bookkeeping software is generally updated annually, so there are many opportunities for programming errors to arise. Knowing that the company has been in business for several years with little incidence of major programming bugs can ease your mind in this area.

Software's ability to fit the business

Entry-level bookkeeping software systems try to be "one size fits all." They allow you to customize the chart of accounts to make sense for different types of businesses. For example, for a computer consultant, it doesn't make any sense to have inventory accounts showing up in the books. However, each software system has strengths and weaknesses for every type of business. Some handle real-time inventory better than others. Some track billable time better. Having a good understanding of what's important to track for your particular business will help you assess which package is best for you — and help you advise clients on choosing bookkeeping software as well.

As you can see, there are more considerations than just price when purchasing accounting software. Spend time to understand all of the critical considerations. You should also ask fellow business owners what they use and how it's working for them. Another important source of information is your accountant. One caveat is to make sure that your accountant is familiar and comfortable with all of the popular accounting packages. For example, if your accountant has worked only with QuickBooks, more than likely it will be QuickBooks that he or she recommends. Not exactly an objective opinion! All of the major software websites have either screen shots of the program or downloadable test versions. This gives you the opportunity to "test drive" the package to make sure you're comfortable with it. Worksheet 2 provides some questions to help you evaluate your choice.

Selecting your bookkeeping software is an important task in your small business and may seem daunting. Keep in mind, however, that most systems can be converted to other systems fairly painlessly. Mistakes are not terminal. Take your time up front in the selection process and you will be making the best decision regardless of the system you choose.

You'll Need a Business Plan

You no doubt have heard it from your banker or your accountant: "Prepare a business plan!" Everyone advises it (and you can advise your bookkeeping clients to do one if they haven't already), but do you know the purpose of a business plan?

A business plan is not simply a document that you cobble together for your bank when you approach the bank to borrow money. It is a living, breathing map of where your business is headed. It encompasses your vision of the business and the steps you will take to get it there. It quantifies your dreams. If that seems a little cold and

WORKSHEET 2
EVALUATING ACCOUNTING SOFTWARE

Ask yourself the following questions to help evaluate your choice of accounting software for your bookkeeping business:		Yes	No
1.	Does the system provide you with profit and loss information about each of your different services (e.g., bookkeeping, government filings, personal income tax)?		
2.	What is the maximum capacity (in dollars or number of transactions) your system can handle? Is it adequate?		
3.	If the maximum capacity of the system is not enough to handle your planned future growth, will the system be easy and inexpensive to upgrade?		
4.	Can your accounting system be converted to another system without having to reenter all of the data manually?		
5.	When you call the software technical support line, are you able to speak to a technician in a reasonable amount of time?		
6.	Does the system give you quick and easy access to your data?		

impersonal, remember that no one gets to their destination without a map.

When I refer to your business plan as a living, breathing document, it means that, as circumstances change, so should your business model. You will have to continually make course corrections as you go along and as you gain understanding about how your business performs over time.

Although you will always be not only the creator but also the main audience for your business plan, there will be others who will want to see your business plan from time to time, including the following:

✍ *Lenders.* They will want to make sure that they are lending money to a solid enterprise that has a probability of success.

- *Key employees.* When you hire a manager or other employee critical to the success of your bookkeeping practice, you will want to make sure that person knows the business plan and will manage the business accordingly.

- *Investors.* Venture capitalists and other potential investors will want to ensure their money will be well invested.

- *Clients.* There may be times when securing a large contract means providing background material on your business, and your business plan is an important document in that context.

- *Potential merger partners or acquisition targets.* If you are proposing to merge with or buy another company, the owners of that company will want to make certain your business is both financially and philosophically sound.

Your business plan should be detailed enough so that readers can understand what the business does and how it will go about doing it, but not so long or detailed that they will get lost in the minutiae.

There are as many opinions on what should be included in a business plan as there are advisers, but Sample 1 is an example of critical information that should be included. Note also that you may alter your basic business plan depending on the reader. For example, a bank may be interested in very different information than a key employee. When preparing your business plan for a certain audience, make sure you have ascertained what type of information they require and what is most important to them. For example, as outlined above, investors will want information on their return on investment. Bankers will want information on insolvency. Be prepared to tailor your plan to different groups of readers.

At first, the sheer volume of the information required for this document may overwhelm you, but take it one piece at a time. All of this information should be thought about and planned out before you open your doors. It may take several months for you to gather the information and do your planning. However, the more up-front planning you do, the greater your probability of success.

Consider Your Exit Strategy

As you're starting up your bookkeeping practice, the last thing you want to think about is ending it, just like it's never any fun to think about funerals or estate planning. But having a plan in place for the

SAMPLE 1
BUSINESS PLAN OUTLINE

BUSINESS PLAN OUTLINE

I.   EXECUTIVE SUMMARY

1. Overall purpose of the business
2. The competition and the business's place in the industry
3. The market
4. Growth strategy
5. Profitability and projections
6. Human resources
7. Financing structure and requirements

II.   EXTERNAL ENVIRONMENT AND INDUSTRY ANALYSIS

1. Geographical operating environment and constraints
2. The industry
3. Product or service analysis
4. Development and operating strategy

III.   THE MARKET

1. Market size in the geographical operating environment
2. Competitive analysis of market servicing
3. Customer group profile
4. Market share growth strategy

IV.   OPERATIONAL MANAGEMENT

1. Cash-flow projections: 12 months and 5 years
2. Break-even and capacity analysis
3. Cost structure of business
4. Profitability potential and timing
5. Operating location and warehousing
6. Operating cycle
7. Life cycle timing

V.   MARKETING AND PROMOTION

1. Competitive strategy
2. Sales strategies and outlets
3. Pricing analysis
4. Advertising strategy
5. Product distribution or service provision
6. Servicing

VI. GROWTH STRATEGY
1. Overall growth strategy
2. Financing plan
3. Growth limitations and constraints
4. External and internal challenges and obstacles
5. New product or service development and introduction
6. Exit and harvest strategies

VII. HUMAN RESOURCES
1. Organizational structure
2. Key employee profiles
3. Ownership and investment structure
4. Remuneration and performance evaluation
5. Governance
6. External advisory team

VIII. FINANCING REQUIREMENTS
1. Amount and use of required funds
2. Current debt/equity structure
3. Proposed return on funds

IX. HISTORICAL FINANCIAL INFORMATION (when available)
1. Balance sheet
2. Income statement
3. Statement of cash flows
4. Ratio analysis

eventual sale or transfer of your business will help to ensure that you operate it aware that you are building value over time. Many small-business owners don't consider whether they're building a business that would be worth anything if they died or wanted to sell. Businesses that rely on the presence or personality of the owner cannot easily be sold to someone else. Customer loyalty is built on that personal relationship.

You want to build the "personality" of your business so that, with training, one of your employees or a new owner can provide the same quality of service that you do. Think about a company like McDonald's. You probably don't even know the entrepreneur who owns the local franchise. McDonald's itself has a strong corporate identity or "personality" that you as a customer are familiar and comfortable with. This is what keeps you coming back.

As you start up your business, think about your ultimate goals. Do you want to build it and sell it for a profit in ten years? Do you want to pass it on to your children when you die? Worksheet 3 provides additional questions to consider.

When you begin with the end in sight, you will be able to aim your business to that ultimate goal and will be much more likely to meet that goal when you're ready. For a more in-depth discussion of exit strategies, you may wish to refer to *Managing Business Growth: Get a Grip on the Numbers That Count* (Self-Counsel Press, 2003).

Selecting External Advisers

The most successful entrepreneurs in the world understand that no business survives and thrives in the long run without being surrounded by a competent and visionary group of external advisers: lawyers, accountants, financial planners, and a board of directors. It can be a very daunting task, though, to choose those advisers. How will you know what their credentials are? Will you feel comfortable with them? Will they align their goals for your business with yours?

When you first start your bookkeeping practice, you may think that this would be a good area in which to conserve your already limited start-up funds. As a financial adviser yourself, you may think you know enough about the financial, legal, and accounting aspects of your business that you don't need to bring expensive consultants on board. I highly recommend, however, that you invest in good external advisers. A few hundred dollars now can save you a few thousand (or more) later.

WORKSHEET 3
PLANNING YOUR EXIT STRATEGY

Before you start your business, answer the following questions about how you will get out of the business:		
1.	How many years do you want to own your business?	
2.	Are there others in your family who may wish to take over your business someday?	
3.	For what price do you want to be able to sell your business?	
4.	At what point do you want someone else to manage the day-to-day operations?	
5.	Will the remuneration and salary you receive from your business plus its selling price give you enough future income on which to retire?	
6.	Can your business survive not having you there or is it totally dependent upon your presence?	
7.	How much of the value of your business relates to its physical assets and how much to less liquid and less definable attributes (e.g., customer lists, name recognition)?	

Different advisers will provide different services, but in general, here's what each adviser can provide you and your business:

(a) *Your lawyer.* You will need a lawyer to advise your small business on many issues, including the following:

- Incorporation
- Labor laws
- Contracts (with customers, suppliers, and employees)
- Mergers and acquisitions
- Estate planning matters
- Exit strategies
- Personal wills and powers of attorney

(b) *Your accountant.* Although, as a bookkeeper, you already have a strong financial and accounting background, a good accountant has experience in the following areas:

- Selecting and setting up your record-keeping system
- Developing your monthly management operating plan
- Defining your key success factors
- Preparing cash-flow projections
- Tax planning
- Exit strategy planning
- Mergers and acquisitions
- Human resource interviewing and screening
- Growth strategies
- Estate planning

(c) *Your financial adviser.* Of all of your advisers, your choice of financial planner can have the greatest impact on your personal and business wealth. Most financial planners can do the following for you:

- Draw up an investment plan for your retirement
- Recommend the mix of investments your portfolio should contain
- Recommend specific investments and even be able to purchase them on your behalf

- Help you determine your insurance needs
- Recommend other financial products, such as mortgages and tax-deferred shelters

Questions to Ask Advisers

You will want to ask your potential external advisers several key questions to ensure that they are a good fit with you personally and with your company. You not only need to assess their experience and skill level, but also softer skills, such as communication style and availability. Here's a starting list of questions to ask:

- How long have you been doing this type of work?
- How many other clients similar to my company do you deal with?
- Can you describe your background and training?
- On what basis will you be billing me?
- Do you prefer face-to-face meetings or telephone calls or e-mail?
- Can you provide me with references?
- How do you see your role in helping my company?

As you evaluate the answers to these questions, you will also be assessing your comfort level with these professionals. Always trust your intuition. You will have to work with these advisers for many years to come, and it's imperative that you feel comfortable with them.

Finding a Board of Directors

As you start your business, you may consider it silly to think about putting together a board of directors. In business news and on television, a board of directors is usually portrayed in a large corporation such as IBM. Every corporation, though, is required to maintain a board of directors, regardless of its size. It may only be a single director (you) that is required. It's advisable to at least have an informal board of directors for your bookkeeping practice.

A board of directors is simply a group of people who help advise and guide the management and owners of a company. Board members may comprise mentors, retired business owners, or others who have skills that can help your business. The incorporation documents of a corporation outline the board's duties and responsibilities, including which issues must be voted on by the board.

In a small company, getting external board members may be difficult, as they will take on some liabilities for the operation of the company, but having them is even more critical than in a larger organization. Experienced board members bring knowledge and advisory skills to the table that you may lack. If nothing else, they bring new ideas and opinions.

Know Your Competitors

Assess what your competitors do well and where they are weak.

Before you start up your bookkeeping practice, take some time to assess who your competition will be. It won't just be other bookkeeping practices, but also accounting firms, tax preparation outfits, and bookkeeping software companies who make it seem so easy for business owners to do their own bookkeeping.

Assess what your competitors do well and where they are weak. Is the bookkeeping practice across town offering a service guarantee? That may be a model you should adopt for your company. Is the accounting firm charging $75 per hour for bookkeeping with no added support to the client? Perhaps you can improve on that level of service.

The process of finding who your competitors are and what they're doing is called competitive intelligence, and it is something every smart entrepreneur does on a continuous basis. It is simply the process of uncovering, analyzing, and presenting publicly available information on your business's competitors in order to maintain a competitive advantage in the marketplace.

Here are the basic steps to learning more about your competitors. For a more in-depth discussion of competitive intelligence, you may wish to refer to *Financing Your Business: Get a Grip on Finding the Money* (Self-Counsel Press, 2005).

(1) *Identify the competition.* Find out both who is competing directly with your services and who is competing for the same customer dollars.

(2) *Analyze what they do right and what they do wrong.* Assess the strengths and weaknesses of your identified competition.

(3) *Determine how they are positioned to take advantage of opportunities.* In this step, you will assess how well you think your competition could adjust to changes in their external environments, such as what might happen if they hired a tax expert.

(4) *Assess how vulnerable your competition is to changing market conditions.* How would your competition be able to handle external threats to their businesses, such as changing tax laws, legal action, new competitors, or theft — all things that are potential land mines for businesses that are not prepared.

(5) *Consider how your business stacks up against the competition.* Once you understand your competitors better, determine where you stand in relation to them based on the same criteria. Are there things you can improve in your business model to make your business stronger in the markets you serve?

Chapter Summary

✌ Before you start your bookkeeping practice, spend time articulating your motivations for wanting to start such a venture.

✌ Plan your business thoroughly and set up a preliminary business plan that projects where your business is headed.

✌ Begin by thinking about the end. Have an exit strategy in place so you will know how to harvest the value from your business.

✌ Choose your external advisers carefully, for they will have much influence over your success.

✌ Gather all the information you can about the markets you will be operating in and your competitors. This will help you strengthen your own business and find your niche.

Chapter 2

FINANCING YOUR BUSINESS

One of the major causes of small-business failure (aside from the lack of financial management skills of the owner) is the lack of adequate capital. The amount of financing you need may be different depending on whether you buy an existing business or start one from scratch. The monetary needs of an existing business will be more easily predicted than if you're starting up a new business. If you are starting your business from the beginning, you'll need financing to get you to the point where the net profits of the business can provide the needed capital to replace assets and grow. Many small businesses start up underfunded hoping that the internally generated revenues will quickly grow to provide financing, but this doesn't always work out as planned. So how much money *do* you need to start up your business?

How Much Money Do You Need?

There are many considerations to keep in mind when trying to assess how much money you'll need to start up your bookkeeping practice.

It's critical that you carefully outline your costs on start-up.

From a financing perspective, it's a benefit that your business is service-based, which means that you won't require substantial up-front financing for inventory or warehouse space. You will, however, need funding over the course of your business for some or all of the following groups of expenses:

✍ *Start-up costs.* Your initial investment in your bookkeeping practice may involve rent deposits, legal and accounting fees, and purchases of equipment such as computers, printers, and telephone systems.

✍ *Shortfalls of revenue over expenses.* You will still need to pay your suppliers and pay the fixed costs of running the business, such as rent, salaries to your employees, and the phone bill, even before you become profitable.

✍ *War chest.* This is simply a fund of money (or short-term investments) set aside for a rainy day or for taking advantage of sudden opportunities.

✍ *Capital equipment replacement.* Eventually, your software and computer hardware will become obsolete and need replacement, as will other equipment you may have invested in.

✍ *Growth.* Expansion of your current operations may mean additional costs related to advertising, payroll, or the purchase price of another bookkeeping practice. You will likely incur these costs before you generate the revenue as a result of the expansion.

Let's start by looking at the two major categories of expenses for which you will need adequate financing in the start-up phase of your bookkeeping practice: start-up costs and providing liquidity to the business.

Start-Up Costs

As part of your initial business plan, it's critical that you outline your costs on start-up carefully and ensure that you account for all of the potential costs. You may forget seemingly insignificant things that can add up to a lot of additional cash you weren't planning to spend. Typical start-up costs for a bookkeeping practice include the following:

✍ *Supplies.* You may not think things such as pens, paper, and file folders are significant, but the initial cost of stocking your office can be high.

✍ *Rental deposits*. You may have to pay a deposit on your rented locations or on any rented office equipment.

✍ *Capital equipment*. You won't need any kind of specialized machinery to run your bookkeeping practice, but you will need the basics: a computer, printer, photocopier, fax machine, office furniture, and perhaps a vehicle for your business.

✍ *Insurance premiums*. Although you may pay monthly premiums in the future for liability or business insurance, your carrier may require that you pay the first year up front.

✍ *Professional fees*. Chapter 1 discussed the importance of putting together your team of external advisers right from the start. This entails incurring at least legal and accounting fees to set up your business and also to retain advice on planning and strategizing.

✍ *Renovation costs*. If you're renting office space or converting a room in your house into your office, you may need to redesign and decorate that space. Costs can include paying a design consultant as well as expenses such as carpentry, painting, carpeting, and sound systems.

✍ *Delay costs*. It is always valuable to factor delay costs into your calculations. Start by asking yourself what costs you will still be incurring even if you aren't able to open your doors on time because of some unforeseen event. If you have hired an employee, for example, you may have to start paying that person when the contract starts, regardless of your delayed opening date.

Once you have tallied all of your expected start-up expenses, make sure you leave yourself some breathing room. Overestimate your start-up expenses by 5 to 10 percent of your total expected costs to make sure you will survive an initial cost overrun.

Cash to Provide Liquidity

Your next most important need for cash once you have covered your start-up expenses is to cover any projected shortfalls of cash before your practice becomes profitable. For example, if you are expecting a shortfall of $450, $295, and $75, respectively, in the first three months, you will need $820 in financing to cover that shortfall.

Many small-business owners who don't spend time forecasting their profits end up having to cover the shortfall in inappropriate ways, such as running up balances on credit cards.

Let's look at an example of how you would predict your revenues and expenses for your first year of operations. Sample 2 is an example of a cash-flow projection for a small business. There are several important things to note as you prepare your own cash-flow projection.

- ✍ *Keep in mind the difference between cash flows and revenue and expenses.* Cash flow refers to the actual inflows and outflows of cash, whereas revenue and expenses (as reported on the income statement) can reflect items where the cash transaction hasn't yet occurred. For example, if you sell an item today but your customer won't pay you for 30 days, this will show up on an income statement as a revenue item, but would not show up in a cash-flow report because you haven't yet received the money. The cash-flow projection deals only with actual inflows and outflows of money. Its purpose is to make sure that you don't run out of money. For a fuller discussion of cash flows versus income and expenses, you may wish to refer to *Financial Management 101* (Self-Counsel Press, 2003).

- ✍ *The "Cash receipts" line reflects your estimate of the actual receipt of accounts receivable, not your revenue projections.* For example, you may collect only 15 percent of your revenues in the month of sale, 63 percent the following month, 18 percent in two months, and 4 percent in three months. As you get more historical data for your business, you will be able to understand your revenue collection patterns more clearly. Sample 3 is an example of what that might look like. Notice that although you are reporting $1,250 in sales for the month of January, your cash-flow report would only show cash receipts of $187.50. Make sure when you are preparing your cash-flow projection that you take into consideration the average length of time it will take to collect your receivables.

- ✍ *All cash receipts and cash payments appear on the cash-flow projection, regardless of their source.* In Sample 2, there is a line for the purchase of capital equipment. This item would not be recorded on the income statement (it is a balance sheet item), but it is a payment of cash. Any projected purchases such as equipment or inventory should be included in your projection. The same would be true of proceeds from a new loan. If

SAMPLE 2
CASH-FLOW REPORT

Small Company Inc.
Cash-Flow Report
January–December 20--

	Jan	Feb	Mar	Apr	May	Jun	Jul	Aug	Sep	Oct	Nov	Dec	Total
Cash receipts	3,725	4,612	4,109	3,289	5,085	5,139	4,103	3,578	3,945	4,210	6,412	5,303	53,510
Cost of goods sold	1,895	2,416	1,989	1,675	2,756	2,708	1,965	1,792	2,006	2,165	3,260	2,585	27,212
Advertising	50	50	50	50	50	50	103	50	50	50	50	50	653
Bank charges	7	7	7	7	7	7	7	7	7	7	7	17	94
Office expenses	61	68	66	72	69	65	73	57	53	65	76	71	796
Professional fees	-	-	-	412	-	-	-	-	-	-	-	-	412
Supplies	39	31	42	19	65	58	17	39	42	58	63	51	524
Telephone and utilities	87	89	79	96	85	89	97	89	71	69	59	76	986
Vehicle expenses	39	47	32	45	49	51	34	31	32	41	39	38	478
Wages	306	310	285	296	314	312	342	284	292	325	312	295	3,673
Purchase of capital equipment	-	-	-	1,953	-	475	-	-	-	710	-	-	3,138
Net cash inflow/(outflow)	1,241	1,594	1,559	(1,336)	1,690	1,324	1,465	1,229	1,392	720	2,546	2,120	15,544
Opening cash	1,259	2,500	4,094	5,653	4,317	6,007	7,331	8,796	10,025	11,417	12,137	14,683	
Closing cash	2,500	4,094	5,653	4,317	6,007	7,331	8,796	10,025	11,417	12,137	14,683	16,803	

CASH INFLOWS

CASH INFLOWS

	Jan	Feb	Mar	Apr	May
Revenue	1,250.00	1,095.00	2,470.00	1,750.00	975.00
Collected:					
Current month (15%)	187.50	164.25	370.50	262.50	146.25
Next month (63%)		787.50	689.85	1,556.10	1,102.50
In 2 months (18%)			225.00	197.10	444.60
In 3 months (4%)				50.00	43.80
Totals				**$2,065.70**	**$1,737.15**

the bank lends you $25,000, it would show as a receipt of cash on the cash-flow report.

✍ *If the closing cash balance on the cash-flow projection falls below zero at the end of any month, you will have to consider how to finance the shortfall.* It is okay to have a net cash outflow in any particular month (as in the month of April in the example) as long as there is a cumulative cash surplus going into the month. This would roughly translate to a positive projected balance in the business bank account, which would be able to absorb any shortfall up to that balance. It is only when the cumulative balance drops below zero (i.e., you have no money in the bank account) that you have to have other financing in place.

On the accompanying CD-ROM, you will find a Mohr & Company cash-flow projection template, complete with instructions on how to fill it out.

Once you have determined how much financing you will need for your bookkeeping business, it's time to make sure that your personal finances are in good order before you approach lenders and investors.

Get Your Personal Finances in Order

As much as you'd like to separate your business from your personal finances (and it is certainly wise to do so), banks and other lenders will be keenly interested in your personal financial situation, especially if you are starting your bookkeeping business from scratch.

If you are buying an existing business, the bank will be able to look at historical financial statements for the business to assess its profitability and viability. With a start-up business, however, lenders generally need further assurance that they will get paid back. From their perspective, if your personal credit history is a mess, it's more than likely that you will end up making your business's credit history the same way. Your personal financial situation may end up crippling your business's ability to attract investment capital.

From your own perspective, if your personal financial life is a mess, you will have even less time to clean it up after you've started your business than you do now. Considering your personal financial well-being and integrating it with your business goals will help you to look at your entire financial situation more rationally and holistically.

Here are some issues to consider when straightening up your personal finances.

Credit History

There are three major credit bureaus in the United States and two in Canada. If you have ever borrowed money (even to arrange a mortgage), you will most likely have a file with these agencies. Lenders report credit history to the bureaus and use the accumulated information to make credit decisions about people and companies. The report will include your current and past borrowings, any late payments, your employment history, and any bankruptcies or other financial judgments against you.

All of this information is distilled into a credit score, which lenders then use to assess how risky you are to them. You should review your credit history at least annually to ensure that it is accurate and that you know what it includes. Any inaccuracies should be corrected as soon as possible, as the corrections may take a few months to show up. Each credit bureau has its own procedure to investigate and correct errors.

In the United States, the three national credit reporting agencies for individuals are —

✍ Equifax, <www.equifax.com>,

✍ Experian, <www.experian.com>, and

✍ TransUnion, <www.transunion.com>.

In Canada, the two reporting agencies are —

✍ Equifax, <www.equifax.com/EFX_Canada>, and

✍ TransUnion, <www.tuc.ca>.

Debt Management

Besides your credit history, lenders will also be interested in the level of personal debt you're carrying. More debt makes you a higher risk. From your own perspective, it's wise to review your debt agreements and interest rates to make sure you're paying the least amount of interest possible and also that you have a plan to pay down your debt. This plan has to agree with the amount of earnings you plan to take out of your business.

Take the following steps to minimize your debt and interest payments:

(1) *Record your debts.* List all of your personal debts, the terms left on them, and the interest rate(s).

(2) *Rank your debts by highest to lowest interest rates.* You will find that the highest interest rate debts are generally credit cards, retail cards, rent-to-own situations, and payday loans. The more the debt is secured by underlying assets, the lower the rate will be. For example, because the bank can take back your home if you do not make the mortgage payments, mortgage rates tend to be lower — because the risk to the bank (not to you!) is lower.

(3) *Review your budget.* Based on this review, calculate how much you can set aside for debt repayment.

(4) *Make a formal debt repayment plan.* For each debt, you should know how long it will take to pay off (not just the minimum payments required by the lender). Start with the debts with the highest interest rate and pay them off as quickly as possible.

(5) *Stick to a budget!* Make sure you make the payments you have calculated every month in order to be out of debt when you have planned to be. Setting personal budgets and cash-flow projections is every bit as important as setting business goals.

Retirement Goals

It's important for every person to review their retirement goals frequently to make sure they're on track, but it's critical for a small-business owner to do so. If you're planning, for example, to retire a millionaire and buy a yacht to sail around the world, you need to make sure your business plan and your exit strategy are in line with that goal. Your minimum financial goal is to be financially independent. Financial independence means that you will be able to live off your financial capital for the rest of your life without working, if you wish. For a more in-depth discussion of retirement planning for small-business owners, see *Financing Your Business: Get a Grip on Finding the Money* (Self-Counsel Press, 2005).

Insurance

Insurance tends to be one of those things you don't give much thought to on a regular basis. It's important, however, to ensure that your personal assets are adequately protected — including yourself! There are four main types of insurance to consider to cover your personal assets.

- ✍ *Life insurance.* Once you own a small business, you should reevaluate the amount and type of life insurance you carry. You will need to make sure your spouse, children, and other dependents will have enough to pay off the debts and live on comfortably if your source of income dries up. Keep in mind immediate expenses upon your death such as funeral costs. Also keep in mind future expenses you had been planning to fund, such as your children's university educations and weddings.

- ✍ *Mortgage insurance.* The purpose of mortgage insurance is to pay off your mortgage balance if you die (and sometimes when you become disabled). Most mortgage insurance policies have inherent problems, however, and you should speak to your accountant or financial adviser before entering into such a policy. The premiums on most mortgage insurance policies are set based on the amount owing when the policy is first set up.

Your minimum financial goal is to be financially independent.

So, for example, you may owe $150,000 now on your mortgage and will pay premiums based on that. In ten years, when you die, you may owe only $10,000, and that would be the amount paid out on the policy. In general, the premiums for mortgage insurance tend to be high compared to the payout. Mortgage insurance can be replaced with additional life insurance for a much lower cost in many cases.

✍ *Property and casualty insurance.* This is the insurance you get on your "stuff" — home, vehicle, and other assets. Some policies also have a liability clause that protects visitors from harm that has occurred on your property. The minimum amount of insurance you will want (and that will most likely be required by lenders) is what it takes to cover the debt that is secured by the assets. So, for example, if you have a car that you purchased for $10,000, and you still owe $4,500 on it, you will want at least $4,500 in insurance, otherwise you will end up owing money to the financing company if you total the car.

✍ *Health insurance.* The majority of people are underinsured in the area of health insurance. It is tempting to assume you will be healthy until you retire, but this is dangerous thinking. If your health fails, your ability to earn income may disappear, along with your plans for retirement. As a small-business owner, health insurance is essential, for you will not be able to rely on any employer- or government-funded health plans.

You need to consider two major areas of health insurance coverage. The first is that you will not have your income any longer. As a small-business owner, you will have to hire someone to do the work you once did or you may even have to close the doors of your business. Either way, you will have to replace your former income.

The second is that you may have ongoing medical and long-term care expenses in the future. For example, you may have to hire a private care nurse to attend to your medical needs.

There are many forms of health insurance. Some include coverage for drugs and dental expenses, some pay out a lump sum when you are diagnosed with a critical illness, and some provide ongoing payments for your lifetime. Discuss coverage with your financial adviser or insurance specialist to make sure you will be able to continue to meet your personal and business financial goals in the event of serious illness.

Sources of Financing

Once you have your business plan in place and you have reviewed and amended your personal financial situation, it's time to look at the potential sources of financing for your business. Although a bookkeeping practice, like many service businesses, has lower start-up costs than a manufacturer or retailer, it is still likely that net profits won't cover the funding of the start-up period. Therefore, you will have to look at either your own or outside resources (i.e., from lenders or investors) to cover start-up losses.

Internal Resources

The most available source of capital, at least in the start-up period, will probably be your personal savings and loans from family and friends. Until your business develops a track record of financial success, external capital providers, such as investors and banks, will be less likely to take a risk on your new enterprise. Luckily, there are many sources of internal capital. Your own resources could include the following:

- ✍ Savings
- ✍ Personal loan or line of credit
- ✍ Remortgage of your house
- ✍ Credit cards
- ✍ Borrowings from friends or family

Some of these sources are preferable to others. Be sure to weigh the risks of each type of borrowing. For example, remortgaging your home puts your personal residence at risk if you are unable to repay the loan. Credit card borrowing is usually an extremely expensive option and can damage your personal credit rating. Borrowing from family or friends can bring its own tensions if payments are deficient or late or if the lender wants the principal paid back sooner than you expected.

External Resources

Once your business has developed a track record of financial success, new avenues of capital become available. Outside sources of funds could include the following:

- ✍ Business bank loans

In the start-up phase, personal borrowing may be all that you have access to.

- ✍ Business lines of credit
- ✍ Business credit cards
- ✍ Private loans
- ✍ Leaseback agreements
- ✍ Business property mortgages
- ✍ Stock sales (in the case of corporations)
- ✍ Venture capitalists
- ✍ Joint venture partnerships

As with personal borrowing options, some types of business borrowing are preferable to others. Some of these sources of funding represent equity (i.e., the lenders own a stake in your company), while others represent debt to outside parties. The type of borrowing you choose may have an effect on the debt to equity ratio of your business, which may impact the ability of the business to borrow more funds.

In the start-up phase, personal borrowing may be all that you have access to. The more sophisticated forms of business financing, such as joint ventures and venture capital, may not be accessible for several years.

If you employ external financing, regardless of the type, there are some basic questions you will have to answer from a prospective lender or investor. The answers to these questions should be found in your business plan.

(a) *Is the business built on a solid plan?* How much homework have you done to prove that this is a viable business venture?

(b) *Do you, as the business owner, have enough entrepreneurial and managerial skills to build and manage a business?* Lenders will look for your training or ability in finance, bookkeeping, operational management, strategic planning, and human resource management. Simply having prior bookkeeping experience will not be enough.

(c) *Is the business built on a model that will have sufficient cash flow to pay its creditors, including this particular lender?* The lender will be concerned not only with their exposure to your business's risk of failure, but the exposure of other lenders. For example, if there are other lenders who have priority repayment or repossession status, the lender who is assessing the extension of further credit may be worried that if you go under, there will be nothing left with which to repay their loan.

(d) *Do you, as the business owner, have enough assets (both personally and in the business) to satisfy the outstanding amount of the loan if you default on the payments?* The lender certainly would prefer to be repaid in the normal course of events, but will also want assurance that assets can be seized as a last resort to cover the outstanding amount of the debt.

Your Relationship with Your Banker

If you don't have a long-standing relationship with your banker, you should establish one before you go to the bank with hat in hand asking for financing. Set an appointment and chat with the banker. Find out about the bank's lending policies and criteria and their philosophy in dealing with small businesses such as yours. Make it clear to the banker that you will be dealing with many other small businesses (your clients) that may require the bank's services in the future. A good banker not only is there for you when you need a loan, but can also provide solid business advice and become one of your peripheral external advisers.

It's also important to meet with your banker on a regular basis, at least annually. Set up an annual meeting to go over your financials and review your lending needs. Your banker may have suggestions for rearranging your borrowing to save you money in interest and fees. Tell your banker what you've done over the past year and how the business has grown. Bankers like to see prophecies come true, and your banker will want to know you've made good use of the funds the bank has loaned to you.

Chapter Summary

✌ Before starting your business, it's critical to project how much financing you'll need to meet start-up costs and to provide liquidity before net profits emerge.

✌ As part of your start-up planning, you need to get a handle on your personal financial situation and make sure it is as strong as possible before launching your enterprise.

✌ There are many potential sources of financing available. Each has benefits and risks that must be weighed carefully.

✌ Your ongoing relationship with your banker is a key factor in your business's success.

Chapter 3

PRICING YOUR SERVICES

After you have laid the foundations for your bookkeeping practice, it's time to decide exactly what services (and perhaps products) you will offer and what you will charge for them. We will first look at what you will offer.

Provide a Menu of Services

Here are the typical services and products offered by bookkeepers:

- ✍ Monthly transactional recording
- ✍ Bank reconciliation
- ✍ Investment tracking
- ✍ Financial statement preparation
- ✍ Personal and corporate income tax preparation
- ✍ Government remittances and filings
- ✍ Bookkeeping training

✍ Bookkeeping software

✍ Software consulting

✍ Hiring of bookkeeping staff

✍ Installation and customization of small-business accounting systems

✍ Workshops and seminars on small-business topics

Of course, you can offer a number of other services and products depending on your training and level of experience. You may choose to offer only a few of the above services or many of them, based on several considerations.

(a) *Do you have sufficient skill or knowledge to provide the product or service?* Dealing with the financial transactions of businesses and individuals is not something you want to learn as you go. Not only will clients sense your incompetence, you will be exposing yourself to potential liability for errors or omissions. Offer only the products or services you feel you have expertise in.

(b) *Is there a need in your marketplace for another provider of the product or service?* As part of your start-up, you will have made an assessment of your competition (see chapter 1). Once you have some background on what your competitors are offering and what services are still needed, you will be able to position yourself to meet those needs.

(c) *Does your business fill a specific niche or can you provide the product or service to a specialized audience?* You will want to assess whether there are specific groups of potential clients to which you can market your products or services. There are two main reasons why this is beneficial to you. The first is that you can generally charge a premium for a specialized audience. For example, let's look at transport trailer owner/operators. Their business issues may differ slightly from those of other types of businesses, but not significantly. If you can learn the important variations of their bookkeeping needs, your knowledge and care will translate into higher billings than would happen with a general bookkeeping practice. The second reason is that it is easier to target your marketing to specific groups of potential clients than to use the splatter-gun approach, trying to be all things to all people.

(d) *Is offering the product or service going to be profitable?* Ultimately, the higher your revenue in your bookkeeping practice is in relation to the time you and your employees spend providing the services, the more profitable you will be. So, for example, if you can bill $75 for preparing a government remittance that takes you an hour to prepare, your recovery rate is $75 per hour. Alternatively, if you want to train small-business bookkeepers and you charge $40 per hour of your time, your recovery rate is $40 per hour, much less than with the government remittances. You need to assess your profitability for each product or service you plan to offer before starting to offer that product or service. You will also need to assess your profitability on an ongoing basis so that you can keep abreast of changes in your business. You may wish to drop some services and add others based on your business's historical financial performance.

Stop for a moment and dream about your perfect client.

(e) *Does the product or service tie in well as an add-on with other products and services you offer?* When deciding what products and services you are going to offer, review them in relation to your other offerings. Some groups of services or products have a natural fit. For example, if you have a client base of small businesses to whom you provide monthly bookkeeping services, it may make sense to go another step and offer tax preparation services, for you know that each of your existing clients will have to prepare a tax return. As well as the benefit of being able to bill more to your existing client base, you will also reduce the need for your clients to seek other (and perhaps competing) service providers.

(f) *Will offering the product or service attract the type of clients you want?* Stop for a moment and dream about your perfect client. What will they be like? Good clients have the following characteristics:

- They are delighted with the products and services you offer

- They pay your invoices willingly and on time

- They are pleasant to deal with and treat you with respect

- They do not have unrealistic expectations and deadlines

- They refer new clients to your practice who are much like themselves

The types of products and services you offer, how you advertise them, and what you charge for them can have a huge impact on what type of clients you end up with. Pricing strategies are discussed in further detail later in this chapter. For now, consider that if you advertise your bookkeeping practice as being the lowest price around, you will attract clients who are very price-sensitive. The problem with this strategy is that someone will always be able to undercut you, and your price-sensitive clients will jump to the new lowest price. Choose your services to attract high-quality, loyal clients.

Clients' Fear of the Clock

How many professionals do you deal with who charge by the hour? How does it make you feel to pick up the telephone and talk to them? How about giving them a piece of work to do?

If you are like most clients of professionals who bill by the hour, the fear of the clock ticking and being billed for even casual conversations can cause stress and even make you not want to call the professional when you really need the help. It may feel like you're writing a blank check. For example, if you go to your lawyer to prepare your will and she tells you that she will bill $100 per hour for however long it takes her, you really have no idea what the final bill will look like. What if it takes her 20 hours?

As you determine your pricing strategies, keep this common client concern in mind. Now let's take an in-depth look at pricing strategies.

Pricing Strategies

There are many pricing philosophies you can follow when you are first deciding how much you should charge for your services. Each has many considerations that you should debate. The main pricing strategies are —

- ✍ cost-based pricing,
- ✍ pricing based on what the competition is charging,
- ✍ pricing based on what the market will bear, and
- ✍ pricing based on your clients' perceived value of the service.

Let's take a look at each of these pricing strategies in turn.

Cost-based pricing

Pricing based on your costs of inputs (also sometimes called cost-plus pricing) involves calculating how much it costs you to provide the service and then building in a profit margin. So, for example, if you pay an employee $17 per hour and it costs you an average of an extra $4 per hour for payroll taxes, desk space, and other expenses, then your cost of having that employee provide services to your clients is $21 per hour (assuming that he or she can bill out 100 percent of paid time — a concept discussed further in the next chapter). If you decide to bill out your employee's time at 150 percent of cost, you will charge your client $31.50 per hour for time spent on that client's behalf. If you choose this pricing strategy, it's important to calculate your total costs, which include both fixed and variable expenses. We'll talk more about fixed and variable expenses in chapter 10.

One reason service providers choose this pricing strategy is the fear of losing money. When you are first declaring your prices to potential clients, you may be afraid of quoting too low and losing money. You might think that quoting higher than your costs will guarantee you won't lose money.

There are three main problems with this pricing strategy. The first is the issue discussed in the prior segment of this chapter: that clients are fearful of not knowing the final amount of the bill before the work is done. The second issue is that your clients can end up paying different amounts for the same service. For example, when you prepare your very first personal income tax return, it will most likely take you longer than when you prepare your hundredth. Using the cost-based pricing strategy, though, you would be charging the first client more than the second for the exact same service. This can eventually impact your credibility as your clients may share information with each other. The third, and perhaps most important, consideration with this pricing strategy is that the cost of providing your services has no relation to your client's perceived value of the service.

Pricing based on your competition

In your initial stages of planning your bookkeeping practice, you took notes on your competition and their policies — including their pricing policies. You may be tempted to base your prices on theirs. You could choose to charge more than they do (i.e., premium pricing),

Buying decisions are based on the perceived value clients place on the service.

charge the same (to stay competitive), or charge less (in order to undercut your competition and try to steal clients away).

Pricing based on what your competition is doing can be the worst of the pricing strategies. First, your competitors' prices have no relationship to your cost structure. Their cost of providing a service can be quite different from yours, depending on their overhead costs and employee costs. Therefore, relying on your competitors' pricing to set your own can leave you much less profitable and therefore less able to continue your business. Second, your competitors' prices may not have any relation to the perceived value to clients of those services, so this pricing strategy can have the same disadvantages as the cost-based pricing strategy.

Pricing based on the market

The strategy of pricing based on what the market will bear is also called pricing at the margin. It is the imprecise science of determining the very maximum that clients will be willing to pay for your services, based on many factors, including how many businesses are providing the same service, how critical the service is, and how wealthy the potential client group is. For example, if the federal government brings in a new law that requires manufacturers to have specialized emission tests done on their plants, then the first environmental engineering companies that are able to market and provide that testing will be able to charge an almost unlimited fee for that service. Eventually, more companies will offer the service and market forces will bring the prices down.

The difficulty with trying to price at the margin is that it requires continuous monitoring of all of the above factors, which takes time away from managing the other aspects of your business.

Pricing based on value

Once you start looking at your business from your clients' perspective, you will see that they do not care how long it takes you to provide the services they need. Buying decisions are based on the perceived value clients place on the service. That value can be determined by many factors, including the following:

- ✎ Speed of delivery
- ✎ Reliability of provider
- ✎ Convenience

✍ Perceived quality of work

✍ Peace of mind

✍ Ability to save the client money

So, for example, if it takes you a half-hour to discuss with your client ways to increase her business and takes you the same amount of time to fill out a government filing for her, she may value the first service much more highly than the second. It has more perceived value to her, and she will be willing to pay a higher price for it.

Once you determine which particular benefits of your service your clients value the most, you will be able to set both your prices and your marketing strategies accordingly.

"Productize" Your Services

When you sell a product, it's very easy for your clients to understand what it is and how much they want to pay for it. They can inspect it, touch it, and test it. The sense of value is fairly objective.

When you sell a service, however, it's much harder for you to market the benefits of that service to current or potential clients. For example, if you prepare monthly financial statements for a small business, all the client sees at the end is a few pieces of paper. It's difficult for the client to determine the amount of effort that went into the work and the quality of the work involved. Someday, regardless of your pricing and marketing strategies, you will have a client look at you and point to their balance sheet and say something like "It costs $600 for that?"

Selling a service involves a stronger marketing and presentation effort than selling a product. One way to do this is to "productize" your services. This means taking your services and presenting them in a more concrete format. Take a look at the following sales copy:

TED'S BOOKKEEPING

- Monthly financial statements
- Bank reconciliations
- Payroll remittances and reporting
- Personal and business taxes
- Business development and succession planning
- Everything you need for your business!
- $55 per hour

This ad is succinct and gets across the relevant information. The problem with it is that it doesn't give potential clients an idea of how much any particular service will cost. Compare it to the following:

LEDGERS BOOKKEEPING SERVICE

Let us help you with your business headaches!

Level 1: The Basics
(starting at an investment of $300 per month)

- Compliance services — what every business has to have done, including monthly transactional recording, government filings, and preparation of monthly financial statements

Level 2: Managing Your Business
(starting at an investment of $500 per month)

- Compliance services — all of the services provided in Level 1

- Management accounting — helping you to prepare budgets and cash-flow projections for your business. We will show you how to interpret your historical financial information and be able to project and plan for profits in the future.

- Taxation — preparation of your personal and business taxes to help you keep up with your government responsibilities

Level 3: Strategic Development
(starting at an investment of $1,000 per month)

- Compliance, management accounting, and taxation — all of the services provided in Level 2

- Business development — we will help you develop your business's strategic plan in order to grow your business effectively

- Succession planning — we will help you to develop and harvest the value in your business so that you can meet your business and retirement goals

---

There's clearly a lot more information being provided in the second communication, even though the services offered in both bookkeeping practices are the same. That's the first benefit of "productizing" your services in such a way: giving potential clients as much information as possible on the services you offer and the benefits to the client of having you perform those services. The second benefit is that the services have been set up in a menu format. This allows clients to choose the package of services that meets their needs best and fits into their budget. The third benefit is that the sales copy gives an indication of total cost. More information would definitely be necessary as to total cost for the size of the client, but at least there's a ballpark provided.

Sample 4 at the end of this chapter provides a detailed list of services from my own bookkeeping practice. Feel free to adapt it to your specific needs.

After you've been in business for a while, you will get a more accurate sense of how much time and effort has to go into the provision of the service so that you can quote a fixed fee with confidence. Even if you do end up choosing to price your services by the hour, it will be helpful to give a total cost range to potential clients so they know the outside limits of their bill.

Chapter Summary

- ✌ Your pricing decisions will have a huge impact on your ultimate profitability.

- ✌ Clients shy away from engaging a professional if they're not sure what the total bill is going to be.

- ✌ You can price your services based on costs, on the competition, on what the market will bear, or on perceived value. Each pricing strategy has its benefits.

- ✌ The more you market your services as if they were products, the easier the buying decision for the client.

LIST OF SERVICES

BUSINESS SERVICES

Mohr & Company is proud to offer its clients the opportunity to choose the level of services you prefer. In addition, we are happy to quote you a fixed price on those services, if you desire.

Level 1 Services

Take charge of your business operations.

1. Telephone or e-mail assistance to your current bookkeeper or financial officer in maintaining your accounting system (such as MYOB or another client-posted system). Telephone or e-mail support on the recording of unusual accounting transactions to help reduce year-end reconciliation of accounts. *If you have a fixed price agreement,* you can call us at any time for advice on these matters with the knowledge that we will not be charging you for phone calls, subject to change orders should the call require follow-up work or research.

2. Telephone or e-mail advice on ad hoc financial management matters to the current owners. *If you have a fixed price agreement,* you can call us at any time for advice on ad hoc matters (brief tax, accounting, bookkeeping, business management, technology, personal financial matters, etc.) with the knowledge that we will not be charging for phone calls, subject to change orders should the call require follow-up work or research.

3. Preparation of compiled (unaudited) financial statements. Note disclosures will be limited. Provision of adjusting journal entries (AJEs) as may be required and/or instruction of personnel on AJEs.

4. Preparation of reviewed (unaudited) financial statements with full note disclosure, as may be required by a bonding company or for bank loan covenants.

5. Preparation of audited financial statements with disclosures to comply with bank requirements.

6. Preparation of annual corporate income tax returns as required by the federal and provincial governments. Preparation of reconciliation of books to taxable income.

7. Maintenance of capital asset depreciation schedule; updating of client-provided additions and deletions.

8. Preparation of other governmental information returns.

9. Preparation of personal income tax returns with all necessary forms and schedules for the owners of the business.

10. Preparation of personal financial statements of company owners as required by banks to secure personal loan guarantees.

11. Invitations to year-end tax planning seminar and other seminars on bookkeeping systems, technology, and business management matters.

12. You will receive our special newsletter and other periodic updates and special reports.

Level 2 Services

Gain control and direction in business and personal financial matters.

In level 2, we help you prepare budgets for profit-planning purposes and actively assist you in interpreting your periodic reports. These reports would include initial key performance indicators that apply to critical areas of your business. We work with you on these reports monthly and totally review your operating plan every quarter.

You receive all level 1 services plus the following:

1. Preparation of annual company budgets with break-even and capacity levels as well as profit goals for desired owner compensation and return on investment. Computation of periodic sales targets to achieve budgets.

2. Setup of our exclusive Management Control Plan and instruction of company personnel on monthly updating. Identification and initial tracking of key performance indicators.

3. We conduct an annual planning retreat for your main managers to set an action plan outlining key goals for the coming year.

4. Basic personal financial planning consultation, including net worth analysis, setting of goals, and calculating funding targets to achieve goals.

5. Pre-year-end tax planning review and forecast of tax balance; setting of strategies for year-end moves to minimize taxes.

6. Review of investment portfolios by our financial services partner.

7. Ongoing periodic analysis and interpretation of financial statements by a Mohr & Company team member providing input as would a part-time controller or part-time chief financial officer, with written or e-mail commentary for consideration and action. While all final management decisions are yours alone, we will outline your options and make recommendations.

8. Attendance in an advisory role at your monthly management meeting by a Mohr & Company team member.

9. Annual Business Performance Review using our specialized financial analysis software to analyze key financial and operating ratios.

10. You may participate in the Entrepreneur Round Table (ERT), a monthly gathering of business owners to discuss topics regarding increasing revenue and profits.

11. Annual calculation of the business's Profit Improvement Potential.

12. Estate planning and/or business succession planning to prepare for inheritance and protection of assets from tax liability.

Level 3 Services

Grow your business for financial independence and peace of mind.

In level 3, we are actively involved in assisting you with the development of your strategic plan. We help you discover the unexploited profit potential that lies within your business. Our aim is to help you make your business even more profitable and therefore more valuable. This will involve us in many non-accounting aspects of your business, including team training, market positioning, and helping you develop customer service strategies that lead to additional profits and more time off for the owners.

You receive all level 1 and 2 services plus the following:

1. Detailed personal financial analysis and planning consultation, including providing analysis of income and spending based on the client completing a personal financial planning questionnaire.

2. Provision of activity-based costing and management of customer base and routines. Setup of detailed key performance indicators and financial and operating reporting routines for client personnel to prepare. Such items will be designed to monitor the key activities that lead to profitability and require less reliance on owner daily input. Client to fax or e-mail reports to us for review and commentary.

3. Preparation of a limited calculation of estimated business value using comparable company sales.

4. Assistance in obtaining an independent, third-party valuation report to document actual company value.

5. Assistance with complete analysis of the Strengths, Weaknesses, Opportunities and Threats for your business, using our proprietary system.

6. We will lead your management team through the Business Growth Program, a unique 12-month process designed to increase company profits and entity value by systematically assessing customer service levels, developing operating plans, systematizing main processes, and training your personnel in client service concepts, phone-handling procedures, problem-solving skills, letter-writing, and overall management development.

7. Facilitation and formalization of customer feedback process. We design procedures for capturing and acting on customer feedback.

8. Facilitation and formalization of team feedback process. We bring together your team to discuss team atmosphere, team empowerment, and team ideas for business process improvement.

BOOKKEEPING SERVICES

Computerized Monthly Bookkeeping — provides you with the following benefits:

- Monthly financial statements and ledger reports in a customized binder for your reference
- Custom graphs showing the key performance indicators that are most important to your business
- Preparation of government remittances (GST, PST, workers' compensation, payroll)
- Guaranteed turnaround time of four business days if provided with all needed information
- Fixed yearly contract price billed and paid monthly by postdated check — no surprises!
- Priced from $195 per month

Bookkeeping Support

- Phone, e-mail, and on-site bookkeeping support to keep your operation running smoothly
- Hourly charge or Annual Phone Support Package

    Annual Phone Support Package
    - Unlimited phone or e-mail support for all bookkeeping-related questions
    - Annual contract price: $99

Setup and Training Package

- Custom setup of your MYOB, Simply Accounting, or QuickBooks software package, including customization of the chart of accounts, invoicing, and check features
- Three hours of training on the main functions of your preferred system, usually divided into two sessions
- 30 days unlimited phone and e-mail support
- $275 plus applicable taxes

PERSONAL SERVICES

Personal Income Tax Services

This is a value-added package of services that includes the following:

- Invitation to year-end tax planning seminar, showing you new ways to minimize tax and maximize wealth
- Preparation of tax estimate in February to allow you to plan your strategies
- Preparation of personal tax returns (US and/or Canadian) including all related schedules
- Consultation to review your tax return and plan for the following year
- Convenient fixed fee — no surprises!

Household Financial Management

This group of services can be tailored to your individual needs:

- Payment and tracking of personal expenses and bills
- Reorganization of loan payment structure
- Preparation of corporate expense reports
- Reconciliation of personal bank and credit card statements
- Budget and cash-flow planning for your personal wealth
- Review of investment strategies and objectives to ensure you are on track to reach your investment goals
- Convenient fixed yearly contract billed monthly and paid by postdated checks — no surprises!

Chapter 4
CLIENT MANAGEMENT

Every successful bookkeeping practice has a work management system that tracks what work is in the door, what stage it is at, how long it has been in process, and when it has been promised to the client. In this chapter, we'll look at how to set up your tracking systems.

Tracking the Work

The reasons to track this type of information are mostly practical ones. You want to make sure you don't lose anything belonging to a client. There are also some "softer" but just as important reasons to consider. Your clients are trusting you as a financial adviser and are sharing their financial records with you. The entire relationship is based on trust. Financial information (whether it is business-related or personal) is considered by most people to be personal and confidential. Your clients expect you to treat their information with confidentiality and respect. One way to show that respect is to have a professional-appearing tracking system so that your clients feel you will handle their records appropriately and with the proper amount of care.

The more staff you have, the more sophisticated the system needs to be to avoid confusion and having work slip through the cracks. However, when you're just starting out, and if there's only you in the practice, the tracking system doesn't need to be elaborate. Let's take a look at the main types of information you need to track and plan.

Work In and Work Out

One of the most basic pieces of information to track is what work has come in the door and what has gone out. It's important to remember that the financial records your clients bring to you belong to them. You are simply looking after the records until you finish the work they have retained you for. Therefore, it's critical that you know at any point in time exactly what records you are holding for your clients.

There are many ways to track this information, but here's a sample of a template for a "Work In" sheet that you can customize to your particular needs. (There's a blank template on the accompanying CD-ROM.)

Jameson Bookkeeping — Work In Sheet				
Date In	Client Name	Service	Date Out	Notes
Aug. 14	Jackson Mfg.	Mthly bkkpg	Aug. 28	- promised Aug. 31
Aug. 15	Kama Marine	Qtly bkkpg	Sept. 22	- held for missing info
Aug. 15	J. Lesko	Personal tax	Aug. 20	
Aug. 19	T. Scaramouche	Wealth mgmt	Sept. 8	- work backed up
Aug. 23	Express Courier	Mthly bkkpg	Sept. 7	- no issues

Such a tracking system will give you an overview of each client's work that has come in. I also recommend you fill out a "Client Sign-In" form every time a client meets with you and brings financial information. Although this procedure may appear time-consuming, it can prevent misunderstandings and confusion.

In a bookkeeping practice, many of your small-business clients will bring you boxes of financial records. When you return them to the client, you don't want to hear "But I can't find the April bank statement. I'm sure I gave it to you" — or something to that effect. Having the client sign the "Client Sign-In" form clarifies for both parties exactly what has been transferred to your temporary care. It will also help you to ensure that you return all records to the client when the work has been completed. You can print blank forms and have a stack handy to fill in by hand when meeting with clients.

Here's a sample of a "Client Sign-In" form that you can customize to your particular needs. (Again, there's a blank template included on the accompanying CD-ROM).

Jameson Bookkeeping — Client Sign-In Sheet	
Date:	August 14
Client Name:	Jackson Manufacturing Inc.
Client Phone Number:	999-555-1212
Service:	Monthly bookkeeping
Records Received:	- July bank statement with cancelled checks - deposit book - July receipts and invoices - July customer billings
Date Promised:	August 31
Client Signature:	

It's important to streamline your client processes, including those surrounding the acceptance and file setup of a new client. A sample "New Client Checklist" is included on the accompanying CD-ROM and can be customized to your own client acceptance procedures. Organizing your clients' records and your in-house procedures will help you to gain productivity and control.

Handling Client Records

While you're setting up your work tracking system, put some thought into where you are going to store clients' records. You will have records in any of the following various stages:

The amount of time it takes you to get new work in the door, process it, and return it to the client is called turnover time.

✍ Have come in but have not yet been started

✍ Are in progress

✍ Are on hold pending further information from the client

✍ Are completed and ready to be picked up by the client

It's important to segregate the records from each other so you don't mix up different client information and return the wrong records to the wrong client. This is all too easy to do when you're busy and working on several things at once. When it happens, it not only gives your clients the impression you're not organized, but also makes them feel as if confidentiality is not important to you. (We'll talk more about confidentiality later in the chapter.) Such impressions can damage your business very quickly and give you a bad reputation in your local business community.

There are many different ways to physically store client records. A shelving system works well, with different shelves for work at different stages of completion. In my practice, we used a shelving system in conjunction with plastic bins. Each client's work went into a different bin with the client's name on the outside. That way, we could always see at a glance how much work we had in the door and what stage it was at. As you are in business longer, you will find a system that works well for you.

Tracking Turnover Time

The amount of time it takes you to get new work in the door, process it, and return it to the client is called turnover time. Quick turnaround time can be one of the clearest (although certainly not the most accurate) indications to the client of the value that they are receiving. Minimizing turnaround time also allows you to be more efficient and therefore able to process more work, which translates into more billings and higher revenue.

To minimize your turnaround time, you will have to track it. You can do this for all of your client work together if you only provide a few services. If your turnaround time varies greatly depending on whether, for example, you are preparing a personal income tax return or recording a month's worth of transactions for a small business, you can also track turnaround time by type of work.

Your turnaround time can be assessed from your "Work In" sheets. On those forms, you will have a historical record of when each piece of client work came in and when it went back to the client. From here, you can calculate your average turnaround time. For example, let's look at the sample "Work In" sheet again:

Jameson Bookkeeping — Work In Sheet				
Date In	Client Name	Service	Date Out	Notes
Aug. 14	Jackson Mfg.	Mthly bkkpg	Aug. 28	- promised Aug. 31
Aug. 15	Kama Marine	Qtly bkkpg	Sept. 22	- held for missing info
Aug. 15	J. Lesko	Personal tax	Aug. 20	
Aug. 19	T. Scaramouche	Wealth mgmt	Sept. 8	- work backed up
Aug. 23	Express Courier	Mthly bkkpg	Sept. 7	- no issues

There are four different types of work in this sample: monthly bookkeeping, quarterly bookkeeping, personal tax, and wealth management planning. Clearly, a personal income tax return should take less time than recording a whole month's worth of transactions, which should take less time than recording a whole quarter's (three months') worth of transactions. A wealth management plan's time allotment will vary depending on how you have your system set up. In this situation, I would recommend tracking the turnaround time separately for each type of work because, for example, monthly bookkeeping, in general, will take less time than quarterly bookkeeping.

To calculate the average turnaround time for a specific type of work, compute the total days between the date in and the date out and divide by the number of client engagements. So, for example, there are two monthly bookkeeping engagements in this sample "Work In" sheet. The first, for Jackson Manufacturing, took a total of 14 days to turn around. The second, for Express Courier, took 15 days. The formula is expressed as follows:

Turnaround in days ÷ No. of client engagements = Average turnaround time in days

Using the Jameson Bookkeeping example, the average turn-around time is calculated thus:

$$(14 + 15) \div 2 = 14.5 \text{ days average turnaround time}$$

You would use this calculation to determine the average turnaround time for each type of work. Understanding your historical turnaround time will help you to provide better completion estimates to clients and will be a starting point for actively working on reducing those turnaround times.

Managing Peaks and Valleys

In a bookkeeping practice, much of your work will be cyclical. Monthly transactional recording will come in the door mainly in the third week of the month, after the bank statement has arrived in the mail. Most quarterly bookkeeping will occur the third week after the calendar quarters ending March, June, September, and December. You will most likely also have clients who only have their bookkeeping caught up annually, as a precursor to preparing their income tax returns. Most of that work will come in the door in March and April, the same time as most personal income tax work will arrive.

The cyclical nature of the work means ups and downs not only in workload but also in revenue. The more the work can be spread out, the more work you can manage with fewer staff. I'm sure you've seen employment ads in your local newspaper seeking contract tax preparers only over tax season. That's one way to handle increased workloads, but it also means you don't have as much consistency and control over the quality of the work your practice is preparing.

Another way to handle workload ups and downs is to entice clients to bring in their work more often. Offer a special monthly rate for clients who bring in work on a regular basis. Offer special rates for one-off services such as wealth management planning in your slower months, like August and November. Spreading out the work and the revenue will help you manage your practice more effectively with fewer resources.

Planning for Time Off

Vacation? Unthinkable! When you're first starting your business, you may not think about spending time away from it. Not taking a vacation in the first few years, however, only contributes to the sense of sacrifice and burnout that many small-business owners experience.

I mentioned the importance of enticing clients to bring work to you more often, which at first seems contrary to trying to take some time off. It's critical, though, to build vacation time into your schedule to refresh and revitalize yourself. And getting out of the office is not as difficult as it sounds if you plan ahead.

Assess when your slow times are going to be. In general, with most bookkeeping practices, the first two weeks of the month will be slower than the last two weeks, so plan your time off accordingly. Make sure that the voice mail message on your telephone and a sign in your office state when you will be off and the office will be closed. Tell clients who book appointments in the weeks leading up to your vacation about the dates you will be away and how it will affect their work. Clients won't think worse of you for taking a vacation as long as they have some advance warning.

Clients expect a certain level of confidentiality in their dealings with financial professionals.

A Word about Client Confidentiality

In general, as a bookkeeper you are not required to adhere to any professional standards unless you belong to a bookkeeping association or have attained another professional degree. However, there are many reasons for you to aspire to the highest professional standards, especially when it comes to client confidentiality. Here are three reasons:

(1) *Your clients expect professionalism.* The first reason is perhaps the most obvious. Clients expect a certain level of confidentiality in their dealings with financial professionals. This chapter has already referred to clients' worries and expectations and the need for clients (and their records) to be handled discreetly and professionally.

(2) *You could be sued for negligence.* The second reason is a litigious one. You may be opening up yourself and your business to legal liability for both the work you do and for the records the client has entrusted to you if it can be shown that you were negligent in your work or your methods. One simple way to enhance the argument that you've been negligent is if a client can prove that you breached client confidentiality. Speak with your lawyer about laws in your jurisdiction.

(3) *Your competitors are professionals.* The third reason is more practical. You are competing with firms and with individual accountants who do adhere to professional standards by virtue of their association affiliation. It is always a good idea to adopt (at a minimum) the standards of competitors whom your potential clients could engage. This is simply good business practice.

How do you go about ensuring that you keep clients' financial records and the work you do for them confidential? Here are some basics:

- Track clients' records and store them separately and away from client-accessible areas.

- Have only one client's records on your desk at one time. If you are going to work on another client's records, pack up the first client's records and put them back into storage.

- Keep client lists out of sight, and never have a client sign a form that also has other clients' information on it.

- When at a client's location, always use your cellular phone to call other clients. If you use the client's phone, the call display feature may show other clients where you're calling from.

- Never discuss other clients with a client. If a potential client asks for a reference, have at hand a short list of clients who have already given you permission to share their names and contact information.

Tracking Your Clients

In addition to having a good tracking system for the work that comes in and goes out, it's important to track statistics on your clients. These statistics include the number of clients, the frequency of their visits, the average billing per client, and the quality of the clients. Reviewing client statistics should be done on a monthly basis as part of your regular monthly reporting. Tracking this information will help you to grow your practice profitably. It will also serve as an early warning if you're headed for financial trouble.

It's vital to track this information because your revenue is generated in three ways:

(a) By the number of clients you have

(b) By the frequency of their visits

(c) By how much they spend every time they come to see you

Your total revenue for the year is: (a) x (b) x (c). In order to increase your revenue, you will have to increase one or more of these variables. I discuss growing revenue more in chapter 11. Tracking your historical numbers, however, is the first step. Here is some information on how you can set up your own client tracking system.

Add Up Your Clients

Regardless of the bookkeeping system you use, it should be a fairly simple task to find the number of clients you have at any given time. Most computerized bookkeeping systems have a report function that you can use to print a list of individual customers.

As you are in business longer, your client list will grow. Ultimately, however, you will want to provide the fewest clients the most services for a truly profitable business. It takes time and resources to properly get to know and be able to service a client. Therefore, for example, doing $100,000 worth of work for 25 clients is preferable to doing $100,000 worth of work for 200 clients.

Compute Frequency of Visits

Now that you know how many clients you have, you need to find out how often they come to see you. If you have a computerized accounting system, such as QuickBooks or MYOB, this information is easily obtainable. From the Reports menu, find a report that details billings by client.

What you want to do with this report is to count how many invoices you have issued. Another way of getting at this information is to subtract the invoice number on your first invoice in the 12-month period from the invoice number on the last invoice in the 12-month period. For example, if your first invoice number in the year is 953 and the last one is 1712, you have issued 759 invoices for the year. In other words, your clients have transacted with you 759 times. This second method will only work if you have issued sequential invoice numbers throughout the period and have not voided or deleted any invoices (in which case you would subtract the number of voided or deleted invoices from your total).

Once you know how many invoices you have issued in the past 12 months, simply divide that number by your client count to determine the average number of annual visits per client. The formula looks like this:

No. of invoices ÷ No. of clients = Average no. of annual visits per client

Using the above example, if you have 759 invoices and 547 clients, then your clients come to see you on average 1.4 times per year.

Calculate Average Billing per Client

Now that you know how many clients you have and how often they come to see you, you need to find out what they're spending. This is a fairly easy process for most bookkeeping practices. Review your revenues for the past 12 months. Are there any billings in there that are unusual and might spike the results? For example, did you have a single client come in with three years' worth of bookkeeping for you to help her catch up on? If this is not a regular transaction, remove it from your calculations, otherwise the averages will be unnaturally high. This process is called normalizing the revenue.

Once you have what you think is a good approximation of your current revenue, divide the revenue by your client count. For example, if you have 650 clients and your revenue last year was $127,500, then your average revenue per client is $196.15. The formula can be expressed as follows:

Annual revenue ($) ÷ No. of clients = Annual revenue per client ($)

One more calculation needs to be added, however, to get to the revenue per transaction as opposed to the revenue per client. You now divide your revenue per client by the average number of times your clients come to see you. The formula reads:

Annual revenue per client ($) ÷ Average no. of annual visits = Average transaction ($)

Following the above example, if your clients come to see you an average of 3.2 times per year, your average transaction is:

$196.15 ÷ 3.2 = $61.30 per transaction

In this example, you have 650 clients who come to see you an average of 3.2 times per year and they spend an average of $61.30 every time they come to see you.

Assess Client Quality

All small businesses — especially service-based businesses — go through it at some point or another. They have to face a client that they just can't make happy, regardless of how much they try. It will happen to you too. Some clients are just destined to complain, berate, not pay in a timely manner, and waste your time. Unfortunately, if you are like most small-business owners, you will spend proportionately more time with clients such as this, trying to pacify and satisfy them. The client is always right, right?

When a customer complains, first assess your role in the situation.

Not necessarily. In this type of situation, the first thing you need to do is to determine how legitimate your client's concerns are. Was there something you could have done differently to either correct the situation or stop it from happening in the first place? It's important to first assess your role in the situation. Even if you were "in the right," was there a way you could have communicated differently to the client? Client communication is a skill that comes with experience.

Once you are confident you are treating clients to the best of your ability, take a few moments and jot down some notes about your ideal client. You have done this as part of your initial planning, but you will have a much better idea after you've experienced some client interactions. What would make a client ideal? Here are some things that might be important to you:

- Paying on time without being reminded
- Being appreciative of the work you've done on their behalf
- Not complaining continually
- Recommending you to other clients of the same quality
- Not being price-sensitive (understanding value)
- Making the work you do for them as easy as possible for you

Pull out your client list again and review it. Place an A beside all of your clients that most closely resemble your ideal client. Now place a D beside those clients that make you cringe when they walk through the door or call you on the phone. These clients are the opposite of your A clients. Of those that are left on your list, break them into two categories, B and C, depending on whether they are closer to your A clients or D clients, respectively.

Obviously, you want to concentrate on your A and B clients. These are the clients that pay well, don't complain, and, best of all, refer other A and B clients to you. Spending your time with the D clients, however, hinders your ability to do this.

What would your business be like if your D clients went to one of your competitors? I know, that's not a very nice thing to do to your competitors! The thought of these clients leaving may scare you at first; nobody likes to lose a client, but think about how much more free time you would have to be able to service your A and B clients. You would also have more time to plan and strategize to make sure that your growth plan is working. Not to mention the fact that you will see morale in your business increase once the "problem" clients are out the door. I have seen this happen dozens of times over — including in my own practice!

So, what do you do about your D clients? Fire them! You heard me right: fire them. You do have the ability to not agree to provide services to anyone you choose. Sample 5 (also included on the accompanying CD-ROM) is a letter you can customize to your own needs to send to those clients with whom you do not wish to do business any longer.

Once you have weeded out your more difficult clients, you will be well positioned to start growing your business with many more A and B clients. The improvement to the bottom line will be staggering.

January 15, 20--

Mr. John Doe
275 Clutterbuck Place
Joshua, MN 99506

Dear John,

There are times when every business needs to take some time to review its interactions with customers as well as look toward the future path.

That is what we have done here at Bronwyn Bookkeeping. We have reviewed the services we have traditionally provided to our customers and have made some difficult decisions.

We have come to the realization that in order to provide the best and most comprehensive service to our customers, we must offer more services to fewer clients.

We have reviewed the history of the services we have provided to you since you have been with us, and we feel that your needs would be best served by another bookkeeper. We would be happy to refer you to one if you wish.

We wish you all the best in the future!

Sincerely,

Mary Anne Jones

Mary Anne Jones
Bronwyn Bookkeeping Inc.

Chapter Summary

✌ It is critical to track the status and location of all client work that has been entrusted to you.

✌ Client confidentiality is a serious undertaking and one that can make or break your reputation in the local business community.

✌ Keep track of the number of clients you have and what you bill them. This is the first step to growing your practice.

✌ Continually assess the quality of your clients to make sure you are attracting profitable clients who are pleasant to work with.

Chapter 5

BUSINESS TOOLS AND EQUIPMENT

In your bookkeeping practice, you will not need a lot of fancy and expensive tools and machinery. However, you will need the basics of any small-business office. This chapter looks at the various tools and equipment you will need, starting with your communication system.

Communication Options

Keeping in touch with your clients and suppliers requires forethought. There are many communications options. This section looks at some variables to consider before buying equipment.

Telephone system

The telephone system you will need is dependent upon how many staff members you have. If yours is a one-person office, then you won't need more than a single phone on your desk. Your telephone line should be separate from that of your home, even if you work in a home office. You will want to be able to separate business calls

Anything that enhances the transfer of information will improve communication with your clients.

from personal calls and turn off the ringer on the business line after hours. (For more about how this may save your sanity, see chapter 6, about working from home.)

I also recommend that you invest in some type of call display service so that you can be more prepared for clients calling. For example, if you see that it's Kama Marine on the line, you can grab their file before picking up the phone. This not only allows you to spend your telephone time more efficiently, it makes you appear more organized and professional.

Also, make sure you have an adequate voice mail system. If you're speaking on the telephone and someone dials in, they should get your voice mail rather than a busy signal so that they can choose to leave a message or call you back. Voice mail also allows your clients to leave you messages 24/7, even when you're not there. Anything that enhances the transfer of information will improve communication with your clients.

Whether you're looking for a single telephone or a phone system, try to get one that has visual message notification. It's easier to see a light on your telephone flashing to show that you have a message waiting than to have to pick up the telephone every now and then to get an audio message notification.

Have a separate fax line from your telephone line. As your business grows, both of these lines will get more use, and they shouldn't be tied up.

If you have staff, you will need a more sophisticated telephone system with which you can transfer calls from one extension to another and call each other internally. When purchasing a system, make sure you get one that can grow with your company. For example, if you plan to have six employees three years from now, it makes no sense to purchase a system that has a maximum three users. Always look ahead to make sure current purchases will integrate with future needs.

Fax machine

A fax machine is now a standard business tool. Many documents, financial statements, and source documents can be transmitted quickly and efficiently by fax (e.g., "You forgot to give me the July bank statement. Could you fax it over?").

It is also possible to get software on your computer so that it can operate as a fax machine as well. In order to do this, you will need a modem and Internet connection. The only downside of this feature is that you can only transmit by this method documents that already reside on your computer. If you wanted to transmit source documents, you would also need a scanner (discussed later in this chapter) to copy the document onto your computer before transmitting it via fax.

Stand-alone fax machines can print on plain paper or on thermal paper. The cost of thermal paper machines is, in general, less, but they are more time-consuming to set up and use and the paper is of lesser quality. One very important consideration for a bookkeeping practice is that ink on thermal paper fades over time and may not last in your client files for the length of time you are legally required to keep client information. I highly recommend buying the highest-quality plain paper fax machine you can afford.

As discussed in the previous section of the chapter, have your telephone and fax lines separate so that both can be used simultaneously. This will become increasingly important as your practice grows.

Cellular telephone

Cellular telephones ("cell phones") have gone from frivolous toy to standard business tool in the past few years. Cell phones give you the ability to manage your office from anywhere. If you are traveling to and from client locations, you can forward your main business line to your cell phone and be able to answer client calls on the road.

Cell phones come with many options, and you should spend some time researching what's available and determining whether an option is something you really need. For example, you can get voice mail (probably a useful option) and you can get personalized ring tones (not really necessary, but fun!). Some cell phones can hook up to your laptop computer to give you wireless Internet access from any location.

Cell phones also come with a variety of calling plans. Choose the one that most closely reflects your calling patterns. For example, if most of your calling time is during the day, you don't need or want a plan that has unlimited night and weekend calling. Your plan should include the most talking minutes in your usual call times for the least amount of money.

Personal digital assistant (PDA)

Like cell phones, personal digital assistants — PDAs for short — have become a familiar sight in the business world. PDAs can help you organize both your business and personal lives in many ways. Some of the common features of a PDA are:

- a day planner,
- an event alarm,
- a calculator,
- data storage,
- a measurement converter,
- an address book, and
- an expense tracker.

Some PDAs even provide wireless e-mail, fax, and Internet access, along with all of the capabilities of a cell phone. Choose the model of PDA and options based on your particular business needs.

Computer System

Electronic storage and delivery of data is becoming easier and more efficient all the time. Here are some general points for you to consider.

Computer

If you are purchasing a computer for your bookkeeping practice, buy the fastest that you can afford. You don't need all the bells and whistles (like a DVD player), but make sure that the computer can handle the bookkeeping software you will be loading onto it. If you're planning to spend significant time at clients' work locations, consider buying a laptop computer. You can turn it into a desktop computer for use in your office by hooking it up to a docking bay, which is simply a cradle that lets your laptop computer function with a regular monitor and keyboard.

I highly recommend that you purchase a new computer rather than a used one. Technology changes so quickly that you need to ensure you have the highest speed and largest storage capacity you can afford. A used computer will set you back technologically, and you may find that you spend more time trying to make an older computer do what you want than actually processing billable work.

If you have more than one person working in your office (or if you expect to in the foreseeable future), consider the networking capabilities of any computer equipment you buy now. Networking allows you to link computers to one another and facilitates the sharing of files and communications. Talk to your computer retailer about the possibilities of networking your system in the future.

If you have employees right at start-up and are purchasing multiple computers, research pricing at not only retail stores, but also computer manufacturers (such as Dell), who may offer discounts on multiple purchases.

Software

You will need several types of software for your computer, many of which you are probably already familiar with. You will need to purchase the different bookkeeping programs that your clients are likely to have, such as QuickBooks, MYOB, Simply Accounting, or Peachtree. That way, you can transfer files back and forth to clients who like to be able to access their data on a regular basis. You will also need a word processing program, such as Microsoft Word, to produce client letters and other documents. Most bookkeepers have a spreadsheet program like Microsoft Excel, in order to produce financial reconciliations and other forms that use formulas. If you produce final financial statements for clients on a regular basis, you may want to purchase a specialized accounting package such as Caseware to make adjusting entries and to produce notes to the financial statements.

As discussed in chapter 1, technical support is an important consideration when purchasing your software. Make sure that the software company has live technicians who are quickly accessible to help you if you run into difficulties when installing or using the product.

Although it is not critically necessary, it is certainly useful to have an Internet connection and e-mail access. The Internet is very useful for research and related document retrieval, and e-mail is coming to the forefront of client communications. You may also choose to design a website, which is discussed in more detail in chapter 8, for marketing and promotion.

Technical support is an important consideration when purchasing your software.

Printer

This is one area to definitely not scrimp on. Purchase the highest-quality and fastest laser printer you possibly can. Bookkeeping practices produce high volumes of printouts, and you will need a workhorse of a printer to handle the volumes.

When purchasing a printer, make sure it holds at least a whole ream of paper at a time, or you will find yourself spending more time reloading the printer than working. Also compare the per-page costs of printing. Some makes of printers have a much higher laser cartridge cost than others.

Although you're hoping your printer will never break, consider this probability before you buy. Is there an authorized repair facility in your area that can fix your machine quickly? You will want as little downtime as possible, so make sure that repairs and purchases of supplies such as cartridges can be done quickly and easily.

Scanner

You may or may not need a scanner when you're starting your practice. The benefit of a scanner is that you can store a large volume of source documents electronically rather than in paper files. If you prefer paper versions, a scanner won't be of much help.

Photocopier

A good-quality photocopier is an important tool in a bookkeeping practice. If you are going to be copying multiple sheets frequently, invest in a model that feeds from the top so you don't have to lay each sheet individually on the glass. If you prepare a lot of income tax returns, for example, this feature will save you time.

There are many good all-in-one machines on the market now that combine fax, photocopier, and, sometimes, scanner. This can be a good option when you're just starting out, but remember that if the machine breaks, you will not be able to perform any of those functions until it is repaired.

Filing System

You will need some way to track and retrieve your client files. Each of your clients will have at least one file and may have several; for example, tax, working papers, special work, and permanent records.

It may not seem important at the beginning when you can still count your clients on your fingers, but setting up a proper filing system right at the start will help you stay organized as you grow.

Many options are available for filing systems. Some are quite elaborate and expensive, like the ones you see in doctors' offices. You can find many sets of file folders in a regular office supplies store that will do the same job. Try to get folders that have been laminated, as they are more durable than the plain cardboard ones. The files should be legal length so that they can fit a range of different-sized documents.

Choose a color for each type of work. This way, you can find the file you're looking for quickly. For example, in our firm, tax files were red, financial statement files were purple, permanent records were green, and bookkeeping files were blue. Buy sturdy stick-on labels for your files so that you can clearly label them with the clients' names.

Office Furniture

You may already have a desk and chair and various other pieces of office furniture when you start up. If, however, you are purchasing office furniture, keep comfort and ergonomics in mind.

Your desk should stand at a comfortable height for you to work at. Ideally, it should have a drop-down keyboard rest so that you type on your computer keyboard with your forearms parallel to the floor and not elevated, as they would be at normal desk height.

Your office chair should be comfortable and provide some type of lumbar support for your lower back. Buying an adjustable chair can make it easy to customize it to your height. Your heels should be able to touch the floor when you place your feet flat on the floor. You may want to purchase a foot rest if you want your feet slightly elevated. If you're prone to tucking a leg under you as you work, find a chair that is comfortable without having to do that, as this posture is bad for your circulation.

You'll need various other pieces of office furniture as well, such as filing cabinets, shelving, tables, and chairs for your clients. Begin your search at a good used office furniture store if you have one in your area. You can find some great bargains there.

Vehicle

You will most likely be using your personal vehicle for your business. (If you decide to purchase a vehicle for the business, check with your accountant beforehand, as there can be some negative income tax consequences.) It's important to track your business use of your vehicle separately from your personal use, both for tax reasons and to make certain you are tracking all the costs of running the business.

Take these steps to tracking your business usage of your personal vehicle:

(1) Take an odometer reading for your car every January 1 (or the first day of your business's fiscal year).

(2) Keep a log book in the car and jot down each business trip. Include the date, purpose of the trip, and miles/kilometers driven. For frequent trips, such as going to the bank to make a business deposit, track the mileage once and then, for each trip, simply mark down where you went. You can fill in the rest at the end of the year.

(3) Keep all receipts for vehicle expenses, such as receipts for gas, repairs, car washes, and so on. You can simply keep an envelope in your glove compartment and put them all in there. At the end of the year, total up each type of expense and write it on the outside of the envelope.

(4) Total all of your other vehicle expenses by type at the end of the year, such as lease payments, loan interest, insurance, etc.

Steps 1 and 2 will give you your business percentage at the end of the year, which is calculated using the following formula:

Total business miles/km ÷ Total miles/km driven
x 100 = Business use (%)

For example, if the total miles (or kilometers) driven in the car are 18,000, and the total business miles (or kilometers) are 7,500, then the business percentage is:

7,500 ÷ 18,000 x 100 = 42%

This tells you that 42 percent of the vehicle's expenses are attributable to the business. You would then take 42 percent of all of the vehicle's expenses (as calculated in steps 3 and 4) as your business usage of your vehicle. In most jurisdictions, you will also claim capital cost allowance for tax purposes. If you're not certain of how to do this, speak to your accountant.

Worksheet 4 (also included on the accompanying CD-ROM) is a template you can use to calculate your business usage of your personal vehicle.

Resource Library

Depending on the types of services you offer your clients in your bookkeeping practice, you may need to invest in several books, many of which can be quite expensive. It's important to set aside money in your start-up costs for this expenditure.

You may need some or all of the following:

✍ Generally accepted accounting principles (GAAP) for your jurisdiction

✍ Personal and corporate income tax legislation

✍ A general purpose accounting textbook

✍ A cost accounting textbook

Chapter Summary

✌ Put some thought into your business tools and equipment needs before making your purchases. This will save you money in the long run.

✌ Make sure you take into consideration the cost and ease of repairing your business equipment.

✌ Ensure that your office desk and chair are comfortable and are at the right height for you.

✌ Track business usage of your personal vehicle, both for income tax purposes and to make sure you calculate all of the expenses of running your business.

WORKSHEET 4
VEHICLE EXPENSES

Motor Vehicle Expenses

A.   Total miles/km driven in year   _____

B.   Miles/km driven to earn income   _____

C.   Business use percentage (B ÷ A x 100)   _____%

       Cost of fuel   _____

       Maintenance and repair costs   _____

       Vehicle insurance costs   _____

       Licensing or registration costs   _____

       Interest expense on vehicle loan   _____

       Parking costs   _____

       Lease costs   _____

       Other vehicle expenses   _____

D.   Total vehicle expenses   _____

E.   Business portion of expenses (C x D ÷ 100)   _____

Chapter 6

WORKING FROM HOME

Many small businesses struggle with the decision of whether to operate from a home-based office or to rent commercial space. Working from a home-office where many of your expenses are already paid definitely saves money and can reduce the risk that would exist if you were locked into a rental agreement for office space.

Many considerations must be kept in mind when you are deciding whether to operate your business from your home or to lease office space. Some of these considerations are financial, while others relate to the effect of working from home on your personal life.

Financial Considerations

Most small-business owners start their businesses with very limited funds, and therefore financial considerations are important. Whether or not you have your business in your home, you are paying the mortgage or rent, utilities, property taxes, maintenance, and a host of other costs. At first it might seem as if it would be "free" to have your business operate out of your house. However, this supposition is not as clear-cut as it first appears. Consider the following issues:

- *Your house insurance may not cover a business.* You may have to get a separate insurance policy to cover the loss of business assets in your home or to cover the interruption in your business if something catastrophic happens, such as a burst water pipe. This is an added expense you will have to factor into your decision.

- *The zoning of your neighborhood may be residential only and may not allow a business to operate.* Check with your local zoning office to find out whether it's even possible for you to operate out of your home. Zoning officials will most likely ask how many clients you expect to have in the house and what type of and how much parking you have available. You may have to pay extra fees or property taxes to the municipality to operate a business out of your home.

- *You will be subsidizing the operating costs of your business.* This will definitely help to save money in the start-up phase of your business, but it may allow you to operate a business that wouldn't survive without that subsidy. All businesses that are built on successful and sustainable models can pay all of their expenses and provide a return to the owners. Your business, if it is to be successful and have value that can be transferred to a buyer, must eventually be able to operate from leased or purchased premises. Not paying any premises expenses may lull you into thinking that your business is successful when it is truly not.

If you work from home in the start-up period but plan to move to a separate location in the future, make sure you have tracked that cost in your cash-flow projections. Am I suggesting that you have to move your business out of your home eventually? Of course not. You may decide that the convenience (which we will discuss later in the book) and the financial savings outweigh the other considerations. However, it's important that you assess your business to make sure it could survive if you had to rent space.

Nonfinancial Considerations

Once you have examined the financial issues related to operating a business from your home, there are some practical issues you will need to consider as well.

The neighbors

Your neighbors might not be as enthused as you are about your new enterprise, especially if it results in increased traffic volumes on what would otherwise be a quiet residential street. If you run a business where you work from home but see your clients at their homes or places of business, you will not have to deal with this issue.

If, on the other hand, you plan to have your clients come to your home-office to pick up and drop off their bookkeeping (and assuming your neighborhood is suitably zoned), it makes sense to discuss your plans with your neighbors first. You are not asking their permission; you are simply informing them as a courtesy and encouraging them to bring any concerns to your attention immediately instead of going to the municipality to complain. Who knows, your neighbors might end up being some of your best clients!

Your neighbors might end up being some of your best clients.

The on-call syndrome

When I first started my accounting and consulting practice from an office in my home, I thought I had set it up perfectly. All client meetings were by appointment only, so that I would always know when a client was coming. This gave me time to make sure my home-office was tidy and that I was professionally dressed. My office hours were from 9:00 a.m. to 5:00 p.m. so that clients could call and reach me during those times.

The setup worked well for about the first week. But thereafter, clients started dropping in: "Well, I was just in the neighborhood and I knew you'd be here." Not only did this happen during the day, but also in the evenings and on weekends. I began to feel trapped in my own home, never being able to spend a lazy Saturday morning in my pajamas reading the newspaper or in my grubby clothes gardening in the yard for fear that there would be a knock at the door. Clients also phoned at all times of the day and night. I began to turn the ringer on the business telephone off at 5:00 p.m. so I didn't have to actively ignore it.

Even if you set parameters on your availability, there is a probability that your clients will not always honor those limits. If you are the type of person who wants to create a distinct separation between your home life and your working life, you may not want to have a home-office. If you do choose to have clients come to your home, here are some tips to make having a home-office easier on you and your family:

- *Have a separate entrance for your home-office.* That way, if you do have unexpected clients, you do not have to traipse them through the kids' playroom and the kitchen stacked high with dirty dishes.

- *Communicate your meeting and telephone policies with all of your clients.* Make sure they understand what is acceptable and not acceptable. Put a sign on the office entrance door with your hours of operation and information on making appointments.

- Be firm but professional with clients who show up unexpectedly. Explain to them (once again) that they will need to make an appointment so that you can be more prepared for their visit.

- *Have a telephone and fax line for the business separate from your home line.* Turn off the ringer on the office telephone when it's outside of office hours. Record a telephone message reiterating your office hours and that you will be pleased to return the call during those hours.

- *Don't feel bad about setting limits.* It will make you look more professional. There are exceedingly few true bookkeeping emergencies that require immediate assistance.

The convenience

So far, we've looked mainly at the downside of working from home. For many entrepreneurs, however, this arrangement works well and allows them the flexibility to balance work and family responsibilities.

Having a home-office will definitely save you commuting time — time that can be spent more effectively on managing and growing your business. It also can allow you to be home when your children get home from school (thereby saving you child-care fees) or when service people have to come to your home to make repairs. If you can discipline yourself well enough, having a home-office will let you structure your day more efficiently around family needs.

The flip side of the convenience coin happens if you are a natural workaholic. It may seem natural to slip downstairs to your home-office "just for 15 minutes" to work on something that didn't get finished during the day. That 15 minutes (especially for a workaholic) can turn into an hour or more. Of course, there will be times when you will need to put in extra hours, but having a convenient home-office can allow you to be overworked and make it difficult to put limitations on your time allotted to work.

Willpower

When you work at an office outside the home, you have a clear division between work time and home time. You know that when you are in the office, you are there for one reason: to work. This is not so clear when you have a home-office, and if your willpower and ability to monitor yourself are weak, you may find yourself doing more lounging than working. Taking "just 15 minutes" to catch *The Price Is Right* or to take a quick swim in the pool can often turn into the majority of the day.

To corral this problem, take some time first thing every morning to plan your day. Make a list of everything you need and want to accomplish that day and prioritize things. Block off time in your calendar not only for your scheduled appointments but also to work on your tasks. For example, if you want to get a quote out to a client by 5:00 p.m., block off an hour (if that's how long you think it will take) to work on the quote. This will help you make sure you are not over-committing yourself and setting yourself up for failure. It also helps you to structure your day so that you are being as productive as you are able.

Time management is important to all small-business owners, as time is a commodity in short supply, but it is even more critical for small-business owners who work in a home-office environment.

Tracking Your Home-Office Expenses

If you do run your bookkeeping practice out of your home, you will have to develop a home-office expense tracking system to make sure you capture the business's portion of the dwelling costs, both for financial management and for income tax purposes. We will look in general at tracking your home-office expenses, but it's important for you to discuss your particular tax situation with your accountant. Expenses are tracked and claimed differently for tax purposes in different jurisdictions.

Here's a simple two-step process to help you calculate what portion of your home expenses you can assign to your business.

Once you've calculated the business square footage, you will know how much of the house the business takes up.

Step 1: Calculate business use

To figure out how much of the premises' expenses belong to the business, you need to calculate how much space the business takes up in the house. First, calculate the entire square footage of the living spaces of the house (including the home-office square footage). Living spaces do not include unfinished basements or attics or unheated garages or outbuildings. If your basement is mostly unfinished, but your office takes up 100 square feet of space in the only finished part of the basement, make sure you are including that 100 square feet in your total living space.

Once you have calculated the total square footage of the house, you need to calculate the square footage of the office area. Start by measuring the rooms used only for business. If you have a room that is never used for anything but business, calculate the square footage of that room (multiply the length times the width). Next, look at the rooms that are used partly for business. This area gets a little gray, so you may want to discuss it with your accountant. Let's look at a couple of examples so you know what I mean.

> ✍ A side entrance and hallway leads directly into your office space and is never used to get to other parts of the house. This area would be considered business square footage.

> ✍ A dining room is used for business seven hours a day and for family meals and activities the rest of the time. This area needs to be split by usage. For example, if the dining room is 10 x 12 feet, the total square footage is 120. However, the room is used for business purposes only seven hours a day. The business square footage is therefore 120 (square feet) x 7 (hours) ÷ 24 (hours) = 35 square feet.

Once you've calculated the business square footage, you will know how much of the house the business takes up. Use the following formula:

Business usage (ft^2) ÷ Total living space (ft^2) x 100 = Business percentage

For example, if the house is 2,000 square feet and the total business usage is 250 square feet, you would arrive at the percentage of the house the business takes up (the business percentage) by the following calculation:

250 (ft^2) ÷ 2,000 (ft^2) x 100 = 12.5%

...siness share with you?
...penses of a home:

...ment, you can apportion a
...s.

...en multiply by the business
percentage (...e is to it. Let's work through
an example.

- A. Total usable square footage of house: 1,845
- B. Square footage of business space: 193
- C. Business use percentage (B ÷ A x 100): 10.5%

To arrive at total house expenses, add up the following:

Heat	$1,250
Electricity and water	972
Home insurance	537
Repairs and maintenance	753
Mortgage interest	6,981
Property taxes	1,412
Rent (if applicable)	-
Telephone (if applicable)	-
Other expenses	-
D. Total house expenses	$11,905
E. Business portion of expenses (C x D ÷ 100)	$1,250.03

In this example, the portion of total house expenses attributable to the business is $1,250.03. Worksheet 5 (also included as an Excel template on the accompanying CD-ROM) provides a place to plug in your own numbers.

Repair and Maintenance Expenses

Repair and maintenance expenses require some further discussion. There are four categories of repairs and each is handled differently:

- *Capital improvements.* If you build an addition to your house, build interior walls, or pave a previously unpaved driveway, you are making capital improvements. These things ultimately increase the long-term value of your house. You do not take capital improvements into your calculation of repairs and maintenance for your business for two reasons: (1) you will most likely be able to recoup the cost of capital improvements on the sale of your home; and (2) there are income tax implications to doing so in many jurisdictions. Ask your accountant; the details are beyond the scope of this book.

- *Repairs that affect the whole house.* Some examples of these types of repairs and maintenance items are duct cleaning, water softener repair, roof repairs, and lawn cutting. These expenses relate to the business square footage as well as your personal square footage. These repairs and maintenance expenses will be prorated based on square footage, just as your other house expenses are.

- *Repairs that affect only the personal square footage.* Expenses such as repainting your master bedroom or fixing the plumbing in the upstairs bathroom in no way relate to the business use of the house. You would therefore not include any of these types of expenses in your calculations.

- *Repairs that affect only the business square footage.* Expenses for maintenance such as replacing carpet in or repainting your home-office space relate only to business usage. You can take 100 percent of these expenses into your calculation. You do not have to prorate these expenses based on square footage.

WORKSHEET 5
HOME-OFFICE EXPENSES

Business-use-of-home expenses

Fill out this form if your primary place of business is your home or if you regularly meet clients there.

A.   Total usable square footage (or number of rooms) of house   _____

B.   Square footage used for your business   _____

C.   Business use percentage (B ÷ A x 100)   _____%

Heating costs   _____

Electricity and water costs   _____

Home insurance costs   _____

Repair and maintenance costs   _____

Mortgage interest (do not include principal)   _____

Property taxes   _____

Rent (if applicable)   _____

Telephone costs (if business using a portion of home phone)   _____

Other expenses   _____

D.   Total house expenses   _____

E.   Business portion of expenses (C x D ÷ 100)   _____

Chapter Summary

✌ There are many financial considerations involved in deciding whether working from a home-office makes sense, including zoning, parking, and insurance.

✌ A home-office can afford you more flexibility in balancing your home and work lives.

✌ Working from home will require you to structure your time to ensure you are being as productive as possible in the least amount of time possible.

✌ It's important to set up an appropriate tracking system for your home-office expenses.

Chapter 7

ORGANIZING YOUR OPERATIONS

Now that you've set up your business and planned what equipment you will need, it's time to think about the actual nuts and bolts of your operations.

As you gain more experience in your business, you will most likely alter and amend some of the policies you started out with. However, it's still worthwhile to formalize your operational policies before you begin so that your policies are clear to both your clients and yourself. Not only will it make you appear more professional, it will help you to stay organized and efficient.

Setting Hours of Operation

When you first start your bookkeeping practice, you may concede that you simply need to work whenever possible to build the business and be flexible with your clients. It is important, however, to set limits on that work, and especially on the times your clients can reach you.

Think about it for a moment. When you go to a Wal-Mart store, you don't expect to be able get in after hours, even if an employee is in there. Established businesses have set hours of operation. You may be fearful to limit when your clients can reach you, but in fact, clients expect it from a professional business. Whether you're running a full-time or part-time practice, set your hours of operation and post them everywhere: on the door, on your business cards, in new client packages. And then comes the most difficult thing: sticking to your posted hours. You may not think anything of answering a client call a half-hour after you close, but doing so gives the client permission to call "just to see" if you are there. If clients know there won't be an answer until the following day, they have the option of leaving you a voice mail message or sending an e-mail message. This will ultimately help you to structure your working day better.

Block off time in your day planner (don't have one? Get one!) every day for returning telephone calls. The busier you get, the more important this practice becomes. Formalizing returning calls to clients ensures that it happens in a timely fashion. A frequent client complaint about their accountants and bookkeepers is that they don't return phone calls within a reasonable time frame. Having a set time to return calls will also save you time, for you can focus on one type of task at a time. In my practice, I always set aside 9:30 to 10:30 in the morning to return client calls. My clients knew that if they couldn't get me right away, I would certainly call them back in the morning.

Booking Appointments

A bookkeeping practice will require you to have a lot of interaction with your clients, not just to drop off and pick up source documents, but also to help your clients understand their financial records and to be able to interpret the "story" that the financial statements are telling them.

As you get busier in your practice, you may find it difficult to juggle getting the work done and meeting with clients. I've already discussed blocking off time to return client telephone calls. This method also works well with client appointments. There will always be times when you have to accommodate a client's schedule, but you can also try to group your client meetings so that you have to do less juggling.

For example, if the majority of your clients prefer morning meetings, your general daily schedule may look something like this:

8:00	
8:30	Operational planning
9:00	↓
9:30	Returning client telephone calls
10:00	↓
10:30	Client meetings
11:00	
11:30	↓
12:00	Networking lunch
12:30	
1:00	↓
1:30	Client work
2:00	
2:30	
3:00	
3:30	
4:00	↓
4:30	Marketing
5:00	

You will also want to put some thought into how you charge for client meetings. You may choose to charge a fixed fee for a meeting, for example, charging $100 for a strategic planning meeting. You may also choose to bill by the hour. If you bill by the hour, then you will charge for the time spent talking with the client. Make sure your clients are aware of this policy, or they may be annoyed that you charged them for the small talk about their children.

Managing time in a client meeting is an art, regardless of how you're billing the client. Once a client feels comfortable with you, it's likely they will talk more in the meeting, sometimes about issues or

If you are charging your client a fixed fee, you will want to limit the length of meetings so you can spend more time on client work.

personal items not related to the work at hand. The art of the matter comes in balancing the friendliness with the efficiency. It's important that your client feels comfortable enough to chat; however, you need to ensure that the time spent with clients is efficient and profitable. As mentioned, clients will in general be annoyed if you charge them for chitchat. On the other hand, if you are charging your client a fixed fee, you will want to limit the length of meetings so you can spend more time on client work. As you are in practice longer, you will begin to master the art of the client meeting and be able to be charming and efficient at the same time.

Quoting Jobs

In chapter 3, I discussed pricing your services. Once you have decided which method you will base your pricing on, you will need to communicate that pricing to your clients.

A common client complaint about their accountants and bookkeepers is that the client is frequently surprised (and almost always negatively) by billings. They don't understand what they are being billed for. The first step in alleviating this problem occurs when you quote a particular bookkeeping or other financial service job.

Many bookkeepers are afraid to quote lest the job take longer than expected and they get stuck not being able to bill the difference. However, such tentativeness will almost certainly translate into billing disagreements with clients. Quoting can be done in such a way that both you and the client are in complete understanding of the scope of the service being provided (i.e., what you're actually doing for them), the criteria upon which you are billing them, and their options with regard to payment (credit policies are discussed later in this chapter).

Take a look at Sample 6, an example of a pricing agreement from my own practice. Note that this agreement is a fixed price agreement. If you choose to base your billings upon hours worked, you would alter the agreement to show that. Either way, the purpose of formalizing the quote is to clarify to both parties the work being done and the amount being paid. Note the paragraph that outlines payment policies.

SAMPLE 6
FIXED PRICE AGREEMENT

FIXED PRICED AGREEMENT

To document the understanding between Mohr & Company and ABC Company as to the professional services to be rendered, we are entering into this Fixed Price Agreement with ABC Company. To avoid any misunderstandings, this agreement defines the services we will perform for ABC as well as ABC's responsibilities under this agreement.

PROFESSIONAL SERVICES will be provided to ABC at a fee of $600 per month. The services specifically include:

- **Monthly Transactional Recording**

  We will prepare monthly balance sheets and income statements from the source documents that you provide to us monthly. We will also reconcile your business bank account to ensure that all financial transactions have been recorded.

- **Quarterly Financial Statement Review**

  We will review your financial statements and analyze variations against the budget. We will then recast your financial projections for the next 12 months to allow you to have a road map to follow.

- **Annual Statutory Returns**

  We will file your governmental returns and information filings for all levels of government as well as any other statutory filings for which you are responsible.

- **Unlimited Access to Advice on Ad hoc Matters**

  You can call us at any time for advice on ad hoc matters in the knowledge that we will not be charging you for that advice, subject to the note below about change orders.

- **Free Invitation to our Annual Client Workshop Series**

  Our annual workshop series includes courses on taxation, business management, and forecasting — critical topics for all entrepreneurs.

- **Monthly Client E-letter and Special Bulletins**

  Our monthly online newsletter contains articles, tools, and profiles of interest to small-business owners. Our bulletins will ensure that you are up to date regarding changes to tax legislation and other critical issues that affect your business and bottom line.

  The fixed price quoted above includes all outlined services. If any accounting or other business management issue arises throughout the year, ABC Company can call us without further charge to discuss the issue. If further work is required, Mohr & Company will provide a separate fixed price agreement for that service *before* the service is provided, so that ABC can be confident that its needs are being met effectively and without financial surprises.

Payment Policies

Monthly payment for ongoing services is due on the 15th of each month and is payable by direct debit from your company's bank account or by Visa or MasterCard. Payments not honored by the bank will incur an administration fee of $35 and will become due and payable immediately. Monthly services may be interrupted by an overdue account, so ABC Company agrees to be diligent and prompt with payment for services.

Service Guarantee

Our work is guaranteed and you are the sole judge of our performance. If, in any month, anything we do falls short of your expectations, we will — without question — respect your right to a refund of your monthly fee if you are not delighted with the work we do and the way we do it.

To assure that our arrangement remains responsive to your needs as well as fair to both parties, we will meet throughout the year and, if necessary, revise or adjust the scope of the services to be provided and the prices to be charged in light of mutual experience.

Furthermore, it is understood that either party may terminate this agreement at any time, for any reason, within 10 days of written notice to the other party. It is understood that any unpaid services that are outstanding at the date of termination are to be paid in full within 10 days of the termination.

_____ On behalf of Mohr & Company

Agreed to and authorized:

_____ On behalf of ABC Company

Managing Work-in-Progress

The term "work-in-progress" (sometimes called "work-in-process" or "WIP") refers to the work you have performed on behalf of your clients for which you have not yet billed. In any bookkeeping practice, but especially in a small one, work-in-progress needs to be monitored carefully. There are two main reasons for this:

✍ Work-in-progress is an asset that will be turned into cash once billed and collected. If you have ever-increasing work-in-progress, your billings may decline and your cash flow will suffer as a result.

✍ The longer between the billing and the work that was done, the less the client will value the work. For example, if your client has a filing deadline at the end of the week and you complete the return for them and bill them right away, the client has a tangible reminder of the value of the work. However, if you wait and bill them three months later, they may have forgotten the urgency of the deadline and the timeliness in which the return was completed. The sooner you are able to bill out work-in-progress, the better.

In your quotes to your clients for proposed services, you may wish to add a paragraph that discusses under what circumstances you would send an interim bill before completion of the service. An example of where this may be useful is if you have started a piece of work for a client and then hit a roadblock because the client needs to provide you with more information and is delaying doing so. In this type of situation, you may want to provide a clause that work-in-progress over 30 days old will be billed and due from the client.

Invoicing Clients

Once you have decided your policies around how and how much you will bill your clients, you will have to create procedures around the actual billings: how they will be generated and how they will be presented.

Here are some important things to note about invoicing:

✍ Make sure that the services listed are clear and relate to the services you quoted for. The clearer the billing, the less likely that there will be misunderstandings.

✍ Make sure that your credit policies (i.e., number of days in which the invoice is due) are clearly stated on the invoice.

✍ You may wish to consider outlining the forms of payment that you accept on the invoice.

✍ Ensure that any required retail sales tax account numbers appear on your invoice.

You have a number of methods available to you to get your invoice into the hands of your client.

(a) One way is to put your bill on top of the work when you return it to the client. This is my preferred method (if the client hasn't already set up a monthly billing). It keeps the connection between the billing and the work completed strong and clear.

(b) The standard method is to mail the invoice to the client, and many bookkeeping practices still do so. However, this method lacks immediacy, as the mail can take several days.

(c) Many accounting software programs now allow you to e-mail or fax an invoice to a client after it has been prepared. This works well as long as your client regularly checks their e-mail or has the fax machine set to "Receive" at all times. If not, then it may make sense to stick to the old snail mail.

When considering how you will invoice your clients, one idea is to survey them to ask how they prefer to be billed. This question could be a standard part of an initial client meeting.

Establishing Credit Policies

Some businesses never have to worry about accounts receivable. Your local corner store, for example, won't let you buy milk and bread now and pay later. This is an example of a cash business. Businesses that deal only in payment upon receipt of the product or service have a more immediate cash flow than those who accept credit.

In a bookkeeping practice, however, it is customary to extend some credit terms to your clients. Extending credit entails some real risks. You first bear the risk that the client will not pay. They will have received their service and walked away, either intentionally or due to their cash-flow situation.

Secondly, and most importantly, you bear the cost of carrying the accounts receivable. You have already incurred the cost of providing the product or service, and you will continue to bear that cost until you are paid by the client. This will most likely require you to eventually obtain financing to fund your accounts receivable. The cost to you of that financing (the interest) is your cost of carrying the receivables.

The third major cost of having receivables is the cost of maintaining and monitoring the system. Receivables must be entered into your books, they must be monitored while they are outstanding, statements of account must be produced and sent to your clients, and you will have to spend time on the telephone trying to collect your overdue accounts.

In setting up your credit policies, you must balance off the projected additional business you will garner from the provision of credit terms against the costs of maintaining a receivables system. There are three main areas of concern when setting up your credit policies: terms of sale, credit decisions, and payment methods.

Terms of sale

Terms of sale establishes on what terms you wish to offer your services. For example, your terms of sale might be cash on delivery (COD), in which case you will have no receivables. Alternatively, you may wish to sell with a requirement to pay in a certain number of days (common practice is 30 days).

Your terms of sale might also include incentives to pay early or penalties on paying late (or sometimes both!). For example, you may wish to set 2/10 net 30 as your terms. This seemingly unintelligible string of numbers tells your clients that you will give them a 2 percent discount if they pay within 10 days, and that the bill is due in 30 days. This would provide an incentive for your clients to pay within 10 days to receive the discount. This also benefits you, as you will get the money in the door 20 days earlier. You will need to decide if the 2 percent in lost revenue is worth getting the money in sooner. In most cases where you have external financing of the receivables, it is worth it.

You may also set a penalty for being late. Your terms may state that the bill is due in 30 days and that 2 percent interest per month will be charged on overdue accounts. This gives your clients an incentive to pay within the 30 days and not be late. If there is absolutely no penalty for late payment, your clients have no incentive to pay on time.

Whatever terms of sale you set for your business, they should be explicitly stated on all of your invoices and statements. When you meet with a new client for the first time, you should discuss your credit policies and/or state them in a "Welcome to Our Company" brochure. The more clarity you have up front about your policies, the less grief you will get later on.

Credit decisions

The second major consideration in setting up your credit policies is how you will determine which clients to extend credit to. You do not

The more clarity you have up front about your policies, the less grief you will get later on.

necessarily have to grant credit to everyone. You may wish to find out more information about a client (especially one to whom you will be providing a significant amount of services).

There are several ways to obtain credit-related information about a client or potential client. The two most efficient conduits of information are business reporting (or "watchdog") agencies and credit reporting agencies.

Most municipalities have a business "watchdog" agency, such as the Better Business Bureau, that tracks customer complaints. This information is accessible by members of these associations. Once you are a member, you can obtain details of complaints against your potential customer. You will need to be most attuned to complaints about billing practices, because these types of activities can impact the financial solvency of the business.

Another method of checking a potential customer's credit history is to join a credit rating agency, such as Equifax or TransUnion. (Details of their services can be found on their websites.) There are rules for obtaining private credit information, and you will have to get the written consent of the client to do so. These credit reports will provide you with a wealth of information about the client's other credit products, how much the company owes and to whom, and the history of credit repayment. This information will help you to make better decisions about your own credit policies with respect to individual clients. For example, if a potential client has lots of debt with a bad track record of repaying on time, you may wish to limit this client to payment upon receipt of services instead of allowing the company to pay in 30 or 45 days.

It can be difficult knowing whether to grant credit to a client or not. Especially in the start-up years, it can be hard to say no to a potential client. However, setting your credit policies will save many hours of your time and effort trying to collect from deadbeats. That's time that is better used for seeking out new business.

Payment methods

You can choose from among many different forms of payment to accept from your clients. Some forms, such as credit cards, have an expense tied to every transaction. For example, in order to accept credit card payments, you may have to pay the issuing company 3 percent of your gross sales received through that method. This fee leads many professional services companies to refuse credit card payments or to charge the fee on top of the invoiced amount if the client wants to use a credit card.

My strong recommendation, however, is to accept as many forms of payment as possible. Make it incredibly easy for your client to pay. Instead of, for example, thinking in terms of losing 3 percent for every credit card transaction, think of it in terms of perhaps retaining that client because of your payment terms.

If you have a choice between having lunch with friends at two different restaurants and you only have a credit card with you, are you more likely to suggest to your friends that you all go to the restaurant that you know takes credit cards? Or do you want to take your chances and perhaps be embarrassed at the restaurant where you're not sure what payment methods they take? The answer is clear. Your clients will feel the same way, and your flexibility in payment acceptance may be one more reason for them to choose you over your competitors.

The other standard method of payment (besides cash, which you will always take!) is a business check. Although there is always the possibility that the check will be returned by your bank for not sufficient funds, this happens rarely enough that it is worth the risk. If you do have a client who "bounces" a check to you, you can request future payment in other forms.

Handling Collections

You most likely don't want to think about having to chase after a client who hasn't paid you, but how effectively you deal with overdue accounts will impact your cash flow more than almost any other management function. In a perfect world, it would be enough for you to state your credit policies on your invoice and the client would happily pay you at the correct time. There are several reasons why this may not happen. The client may simply be a deadbeat without any intention to pay. The sooner you are aware of this and take action, the more likely you will see some cash eventually.

The client may be distracted and only pay attention to the bill when they have received a statement of account. In this case, the sooner you get statements of account out the door, the sooner cash will come in the door. Some clients may be using you as an unwitting source of financing. They may routinely take 60 or 90 days to pay their suppliers, working on the premise that most suppliers will let the receivables go that long before they get serious about collection.

You should take some time in the beginning to determine your collection policy and ensure that your clients are aware of it. For example, if your terms are net 30 days, you may wish to send out a statement of account at the beginning of every month for all customers that have outstanding invoices. This will include clients whose invoices are not yet due, but it will be a gentle reminder to them of when their invoice needs to be paid. Statements that are prepared for clients with accounts over 30 days should have a bright sticker or other indication on them that action needs to be taken. In many cases, this will be enough to get the account paid.

At 60 days overdue, you may wish to call the client directly and discuss the invoice. As much as you may not want to discuss the outstanding invoice with your clients, they will want to discuss it even less, and this may prompt them to pay the bill. At 90 days, you may wish to turn the account over to a collection agency to recover the funds. It will make your life much easier to be able to concentrate on clients who pay on time and let professionals deal with the deadbeats. They're good at it and they do it for a living.

Chapter Summary

✌ Setting your operational policies before you start up your business will help you to be efficient.

✌ Don't be afraid to put your quotes in writing to your clients. Just ensure that situations where the price may change are clearly stated.

✌ Accepting as many forms of payment as possible can give you a competitive edge over your competition.

✌ Your most effective weapons in collecting your accounts receivable are regular billing and monthly statements.

Chapter 8

MARKETING AND PROMOTION

Developing an effective marketing and promotion strategy for your bookkeeping business can mean the difference between a growing and thriving business and a stagnating one. As a new business owner, you will find yourself inundated with advertising opportunities, including print, radio, and perhaps even television. Before you take the leap and spend significant financial resources on ads for your business, you need to understand both the content of your advertising message and the best way to reach your potential clients.

Finding Your Niche

The first step in determining your advertising message is to discover your business's niche. Finding your niche means determining the services you offer, to whom you offer them, and your method of offering them in comparison to your competitors. How is your business different from that of your competition? What benefits and value will your clients get from your services?

What makes you stand out
from your competitors?

Consumer theory shows that clients buy value that they perceive. What this means is that if they feel that the benefits of your services outweigh their cost by a higher margin than your competitors', then they will buy that perceived value. The value to a client is defined as "Benefits ÷ Price."

For example, if your clients perceive that they can get the same benefits from a different bookkeeping business for a lower price than you charge, they will be inclined to go with the lower price. However, if you are able to present the benefits your service offers that your competition doesn't, your clients will factor in the added benefits they will be receiving when they evaluate your pricing structure.

Articulating the value of your services, however, runs much deeper than simply a slogan. It needs to be at the heart of your business. It is embedded in your vision and mission statements, and it needs to be communicated indirectly to clients through every interaction you have with them.

Does the value you offer to clients have to be completely different from that offered by any other business in your industry? Of course not. You simply have to articulate it more effectively.

For example, FedEx's value statement (and in fact the core of their entire business) is "Absolutely Positively Overnight." Are they the only courier company on the planet that can deliver packages overnight? Of course not! But they articulate it better than anyone else. It's clear to their customers and potential customers that they will get it there by tomorrow morning. And, of course, that's extremely important to customers of the courier industry.

So, how can you articulate the value that your business provides? What makes you stand out from your competitors? Are you the most experienced bookkeeper? Do you offer the most services?

Let's take a look at some other famous value statements and the values they articulate:

- New York Life: "The Company You Keep" (longevity)

- Chrysler: "Inspiration Comes Standard" (creativity, value)

- Purina: "Your Pet, Our Passion" (dedication, attention to detail)

At first, these may seem nothing more than advertising slogans. And, in fact, they are used as such. But these are core values — the basis upon which these companies set their operating policies. Keeping your value statement short and easy to remember helps embed it in the minds of both clients and employees.

Once you have determined your value statement, make sure it permeates all your correspondence and internal processes and procedures. Make it the very core of your operations.

Articulating the value of a service can be more difficult than articulating the value of a product. A product is tangible; it is something a customer can touch, see, and smell. A service, on the other hand, is intangible. When it has been completed, the client may be hard-pressed to know what value has been added. Therefore it's critical that you define and communicate the value of your services.

Pricing Is Key

Chapter 3 discussed setting your pricing structure. This chapter links pricing to marketing, because, ultimately, your pricing strategy is part of your marketing strategy, not simply an administrative task.

The marketing question that you need to ask yourself is, "Why should clients use my services?" What is it that makes you different and makes you stand out from your competitors? You've already discovered what niche you inhabit. Now we have to link pricing to your niche. There really are only two bases upon which you can compete in business: price and value.

Competing on price

"THE LOWEST PRICE IN TOWN." "WE MATCH ALL COMPETITORS' PRICES." "NOBODY BEATS US . . . NOBODY!" I'm sure you've seen headlines like this in the advertising section of your local newspaper. In fact, take a few minutes right now and look through the sales flyers in the newspaper. How many businesses are advertising that their price is the best?

Many small businesses (especially new ones) feel they have to compete on price alone, that customers will only buy from them if they offer the cheapest goods or services. However, setting prices that are too low only starts a downward cycle, where each business in an industry undercuts the other until there are no margins left, and businesses start going bankrupt or leaving the industry. The airline industries in both the United States and Canada are excellent examples of this dysfunctional strategy.

If you think you can undercut all your competitors, think again. There will always be new competitors in the market who can undercut you. New competitors have the benefit of still having their start-up financing in place and can price almost at cost for however long they feel it will take to yank your client base out from under you.

Something else to consider is that the type of client that buys from you solely on price will jump to a competitor in a heartbeat if the competitor's prices are lower. There is no client loyalty at this end of the market. It can make for some very hard slogging on your part just to keep solvent if you are going to compete on price.

Competing on value

The other strategy upon which to base your pricing is by adding value. By far the largest segment of clients doesn't simply want the cheapest price regardless. This is especially true with a financial service. Clients understand that this service is not simply a commodity; it is a value-added service. They want to know that they are getting value for their money. It's not that they want to pay more if they don't have to, but they understand that cheaper isn't always better. Once again, clients define value as:

Benefits ÷ Price

The higher the perceived benefits to the clients versus the price of a service, the more likely they are to purchase that service. Notice that we are speaking of "perceived benefits." That means the clients need to believe they are getting the best product or service for the best price. Conveying that value perception to clients is one of your most important jobs.

My experience has shown me that most small businesses are terrified to compete on value, because it is so ingrained in them that they have to cut prices to stay in business. But think about how wonderful it would be to get a higher price for your services, provide better-quality service to your clients, and have them appreciate what you provide to them. That's the outcome of competing on value.

Presenting Your Best Self

When you think about marketing and promotion, you may first think about advertising, but promoting your business goes much farther than that. Your promotional strategy stems from your vision for your business and the niche in which you choose to operate. Once those have been defined, every interaction you and your business have with the outside world should portray that image. Let's take a look at some ways you can communicate your firm's marketing message.

How you dress

Every professional has a different idea of what clothes are appropriate for business. Certainly, if you're doing client work at your dining-room table at midnight, it's okay to be in your Winnie-the-Pooh pajamas. But meeting with clients is another matter entirely. Keep in mind that the goal is to make the client feel comfortable. In many instances, dressing in a three-piece suit is not what will make a client feel comfortable and feel that you are warm and approachable.

Some client situations will clearly dictate the appropriate clothes. For example, if you are meeting a house-building client at his construction site, you will want to wear clothing appropriate for that venue, perhaps a dress shirt and jeans. On the other hand, if your client is a funeral director, you will want to make sure you dress in a similar fashion to her, which will most likely mean simple dress clothes in dark colors. When dressing for the office, always keep client perceptions in mind.

How you answer the telephone

The way you and your staff answer the business phones can either garner or turn away new clients. It can either make existing clients feel valued or make them feel bothersome. When you are bogged down in the day-to-day operation of your business, you may not put much thought into your tone or how your staff answers the phone, but these simple things can communicate a lot about your business.

As an example, look at the following different ways your receptionist can answer the same telephone call:

Example A.

"Hi, Jameson Bookkeeping."

"Anita? Ah, she's busy right now. Can I take a message?"

Example B.

"Hi, Jameson Bookkeeping. This is Janet Mackie."

"Anita is with someone at the moment. Is there anything I can do to help?"

You may think these are very small differences in the way the telephone is answered, but think about which business you'd rather deal with if you were a potential client. In the first scenario, you are told that Anita is busy (too busy for new clients?). Then you are invited to leave a message for her. This effectively cuts off any further communication the potential client might want to engage in. It is likely that they will leave a message and then call the next bookkeeping firm in the phone book.

In the second scenario, even though Anita still cannot answer the call, the reason why is less grating. Of course she might be with someone if she runs a successful bookkeeping practice. The receptionist not only introduces herself to the caller (a great way of inviting the caller to do the same) but also offers to help. This opens up the lines of communication and comes across as friendly and helpful. Even if Janet is unable to ultimately help the caller, she can then let the caller know that Anita can answer all of the caller's questions as soon as she's free. This one change in telephone manner can have a huge impact on your bottom line.

Have a telephone script for each staff member (including yourself) to follow to make sure that a consistent communication happens every time the telephone is answered.

How you decorate your office

In addition to your telephone manners, your office also speaks volumes about you and your business. If your office is always a mess and has stacks of files and papers all over the place, it conveys the sense that you are disorganized and unprofessional. If, on the other hand, it is warm and inviting, it conveys comfort to clients.

Take a look at your office from a client's perspective. It's easy to get "office blind" — where you don't see the mess any more. Try to see what a client sees and make your office as clean and inviting as possible (and, of course, make sure that all client files are tucked away out of sight).

Advertising with a Purpose

Before you begin to take out advertisements in telephone directories, newspapers, magazines, and every other place someone wants to sell you a spot, take some time to determine the purpose of your advertising. What do you want from it? The main purpose of any advertising for a commercial business is to get a response. You want potential clients to read your ad and immediately pick up the telephone and call to book an appointment.

So, how do you make sure your advertising accomplishes that? Someone once said, "I know I'm wasting half of my advertising money. I just don't know which half." The first critical thing you need to do is to set up a system to track the results of your advertising. You will spend far less and your ads will be far more effective if you direct your advertising dollars into those areas where you know you'll be successful.

Print and radio advertising can be the most expensive part of your marketing and promotion campaign. And if you're large enough to have a television advertising budget, the cost can be astronomical. It makes little sense, then, that most small businesses never know what benefits, if any, they are getting from their advertising campaigns. The cost of this ignorance can be enormous.

Let's start with the basics: Do you know where your new clients are coming from now? Telephone book ads? Word of mouth? Networking? For example, let's say you were spending $2,000 per year to have a display ad in the telephone book. Through analyzing your client base and finding out where clients first heard about your business, you discover that only 3 percent of your clients found you in the telephone book. Most of your clients came in through referrals from existing clients or other associates. What impact will this have on your advertising budget? Are you likely to spend $2,000 next year to get only a few more clients? Not likely. You will have saved $2,000 and will still have almost the same number of customers. This illustrates why testing and measuring the results of your advertising campaigns can be very lucrative for your business.

Once you know where your clients are coming from, you can then analyze the effectiveness of how you market to them. If most of your clients come in through referrals, one of your growth strategies may be to actively pursue your business contacts to solicit referrals. It's important to know how effective this change has been on

Most small businesses never know what benefits, if any, they are getting from their advertising campaigns.

your number of clients and your revenue. For example, let's say you send a mailing to your existing clients with a business card and an offer of 50 percent off their next visit to you if they bring in a new client. It's then a very simple matter of tracking how many new clients come in as referrals of existing clients.

If your appeal only results in one new client for every 100 letters you send to existing clients, you know that the campaign has not been very effective. This will let you modify the campaign to improve its effectiveness. Try it again with 75 percent off the next visit or change the wording of the letter. But remember to only change one variable at a time so that you know when you've hit upon a winning combination.

This approach also works with print, radio, and television advertising. Every piece of advertising should be measurable. It is a marketing truism that different headlines can have a dramatic impact on customer response. Test the effectiveness of your headlines, make changes, then test them again. See how many responses the ads elicit and what the conversion ratio is. (For a more detailed discussion of conversion ratio, you may wish to refer to *Managing Business Growth*, Self-Counsel Press, 2003.)

So, how are you able to determine your best advertising strategy? The important point here is to proceed slowly. Most financial service clients come through referral, not through expensive and flashy advertising. Start to build your network of business contacts, either formally, through a networking group like your local chamber of commerce, or informally, through bankers, lawyers, and other business owners. Building these networks may seem like a very long and tedious process, but it will ultimately result in steadily increasing business.

As you start to get more clients, remind them that you are still looking for more business. If they are pleased with your service, they will be happy to refer others to you.

If you do choose to advertise in print, make sure you include lots of information in your ad. Don't go for flashy with lots of blank space. That may work for some types of businesses, but your potential clients will want all the information they can get in a low-pressure environment. If they have to pick up the telephone to ask you questions about your services and policies, they might shy away, fearing that you will try to hard-sell them over the phone. More information in an advertisement for bookkeeping services is always better. Consider this bookkeeping ad:

More Than Just Bean Counters
Garden City Bookkeeping Services

We solve business problems for:

- Individuals
- Businesses
- Charities
- Farms

Fixed fees — you always know what you will pay up front

Guaranteed turnaround time — never wait for your work again!

Tiered services — choose only the services you need from our "menu"

No-charge initial consultation — come meet with us and let us show you how we're different

Call us today!
(555) 555-1234

Should You Have a Website?

These days, many businesses have websites for promotional purposes. You may wish to consider setting one up for the following reasons:

- *To serve as an online brochure.* Having all of your advertising and promotional information online will be more cost-effective than printing full-color brochures. You can also include much more detail than you could in print format.

- *To publish articles and links to other resources for your clients.* This positions you as an expert in your field and increases your credibility.

- *To publish client testimonials.* Every potential client wants to hear how your existing clients feel about you and the service you provide.

- *To provide an easy e-mail link for potential clients to reach you.* The easier you make it for potential clients to get in touch with you, the more likely they will.

✍ *To allow clients to sign up for an e-newsletter*. Sending periodic newsletters via e-mail is more cost-effective that sending them by regular mail. You can also track statistics on how many people opened the e-newsletter, which parts were read the most often, and which days you get the best response. You can also send out special offers and packages via your e-newsletter.

✍ *To convey the stability of your bookkeeping practice*. A website shows that you are committed to your business and care about your clients. It shows that you are established and in business for the long term.

Keeping Your Current Clients Happy

It's true that it costs less to keep the clients you have than to get new ones. When you are trying to build your business, you may have a natural tendency to focus all of your energy on potential clients, not the ones you already have. Remember, though, that most of your new business will come from referrals from your existing client base, so make sure every interaction with your clients shows that you are committed to them.

There are many seemingly small (and free!) ways to make your clients feel comfortable and welcome. Here are some tips:

✍ *Take a few seconds before picking up the telephone and smile*. The warmth will come across in your voice, and you are less likely to transmit stress and "being busy" to your client.

✍ *Focus your attention completely on a client when meeting with them*. Turn off the ringer on the telephone, don't touch your cell phone or PDA, and don't rifle through papers. Make eye contact and echo back what your client is telling you. This conveys the sense that you are truly listening to them.

✍ *Always under-promise and over-deliver*. Don't let rain, snow, sleet, or hail make you miss your deadlines. If you know that you have to miss a promised date, call your client as soon as possible to discuss the delay.

✍ *Show up for meetings on time*. If you are prone to being chronically late (like me!), build in some safety measures such as turning your watch ahead by ten minutes or booking the appointment in your day planner fifteen minutes earlier than it is. (My administrative assistant did this without me knowing for almost a year — and it worked!)

✍ *Keep your office tidy and inviting for clients.* Clients make many silent judgments about you based on things such as the state of your office, your clothes, and your car. Make sure your office and you yourself portray a professional image at all times.

✍ *Actively solicit feedback from your clients.* In our firm, we sent out a feedback form with every year-end financial statement engagement that we did. My entire staff took pride in reading them and finding out the things about our firm that the clients liked. It also gave our clients the opportunity to discuss what they didn't like in a nonconfrontational way so that we could address those issues and improve our service. Sample 7 (also included on the accompanying CD-ROM) is a copy of the feedback form we used in our firm. You can adapt this to your particular needs.

Chapter Summary

✌ Defining what sets your business apart from your competitors drives your entire marketing and promotion strategy.

✌ How you present yourself and your business conveys lots of information — both positive and negative — to your clients and potential clients.

✌ Ensure that every advertising and marketing campaign you engage in can be tracked to see how effective it is.

✌ Don't sacrifice your current clients in the pursuit of new ones. It's less expensive to retain clients than to have to replace them.

CLIENT SATISFACTION SURVEY

Thank you for taking the time to complete this brief survey. It will help us serve you better in the future!

Business Name:_____
(you may remain anonymous if you wish)

Please rate the following items on a scale of 1 to 5 using the equivalents below:

1 = unhappy
3 = satisfied
5 = delighted

		1	2	3	4	5
Greetings						
1	How were you greeted on the telephone?	1	2	3	4	5
2	Were your calls returned promptly?	1	2	3	4	5
3	Were your e-mails responded to promptly?	1	2	3	4	5
4	How well were you greeted in the office?	1	2	3	4	5
5	Were you offered coffee, tea, or water?	1	2	3	4	5
Work Completion						
6	Was the turnaround time acceptable?	1	2	3	4	5
7	Were your year-end results explained to you?	1	2	3	4	5
8	Were your questions answered fully?	1	2	3	4	5
9	Did we follow up promptly on any outstanding issues?	1	2	3	4	5
10	Did we explain the 5% discount for prompt payment?	1	2	3	4	5

Questions

Is there anything else you feel we can improve upon?

Is there anything that you particularly enjoyed about your contact with us? (i.e., things we shouldn't change)

Are there any other services you feel we should be providing to our clients?

Thanks for your input! It will be reviewed carefully. Please return survey in the enclosed envelope.

Chapter 9

HAVING EMPLOYEES

You may wish to forever run your bookkeeping practice on your own. However, in order for the business to run in your absence or to have value that can ultimately be sold or passed on to the next generation, you will have to hire help at some point. Human resource management can be one of the most difficult tasks for any small-business owner. More likely than not, you have never received any kind of training in hiring, firing, and managing employees.

You will want to dedicate some time to learning about the compensation process. Many textbooks and courses are available on human resource management. It is an important and separate skill set distinct from all others you use in your business. The goal of this chapter is to give you an overview of the hiring and compensation process and guide you to paying your employees what they're worth.

Spending time working on the compensation process provides dual benefits: it makes your employees stay longer (because you are paying them what they're worth) and it makes you more money (because you are paying them based on their performance).

Before you hire, decide what you need that person to do.

Hiring 101

When should you start looking for an employee? There are several road markers that will tell you it's time to find someone to work for you. Watch for the following signs:

- ✍ Your revenue would increase by more than the additional payroll expense if you were able to concentrate on your strengths (i.e., getting more work in the door).

- ✍ You are unable to spend at least 20 percent of your time working *on* your business in planning and strategizing activities.

- ✍ You do not have the time to implement the marketing and promotion plan that's required to achieve your projected growth.

- ✍ You are approaching your capacity with regards to labor input (i.e., you have more work than hours available in which to do it).

- ✍ You are spending money on late fees and penalties because you cannot stay on top of the accounts payable and the required government filings.

- ✍ You begin to feel tired and burned out all of the time. You will notice the impact of this state fairly quickly, for your productivity will decline drastically.

Any one of these indicators requires that you consider hiring additional staff. Before you hire, however, you will have to decide what you need that person to do.

Building a job description

There are many different ways to decide what you want your new employee or employees to do. You could have them look after the things you're not getting around to doing, the things you're not very good at doing, or the things you don't like doing.

The first step in deciding what you want your new employee to do is to outline all the "jobs" in your business. You may not have thought about your business as having several different jobs because you are the only one doing them. It may seem like one super-sized job to you. Separating out the functions, however, will help you to decide what needs to be done.

Jobs are simply a collection of processes. These processes can be grouped together into natural clusters relating to an employee's job responsibilities. Here are some of the common processes:

- ✍ Accounts receivable (billing, collection, tracking, cash handling)

- ✍ Accounts payable (tracking, check production)

- ✍ Office support (answering calls, greeting clients, booking appointments, filing, making coffee)

- ✍ Sales (customer presentations, follow-up, cold-calling, trade shows and networking groups)

- ✍ Marketing and promotion (managing advertising, designing marketing tools, writing ad copy and customer letters)

- ✍ Production (doing client work)

- ✍ Operations management (overseeing the production process, supervising employees, reporting on operations)

Once you have outlined what the processes are in your practice, it's time to document them. This will clarify for you and your employee what the expectations of the job are. Sample 8 (also on the accompanying CD-ROM) is a documentation of the accounts receivable process in a small pest control company. You can modify and customize it as you need to create your own template. Note that in a small business, this process likely would not take enough time to be a full-time job. It would be combined with other processes to form an employee's workload.

Once you have outlined all the processes in your business, take some time to honestly assess your own strengths and weaknesses. Are you good at client work but not so good at booking appointments? Are you skilled at putting together a detailed budget but not at handling customer complaints? The goal here is to assign to yourself the set of processes where you add the most value to the business and hire someone to do a great job at the processes where you are the weakest.

The laws of the land

Now you know what skill set you are looking for. Great! But before you place that first ad for a new employee, it's important to understand your rights and responsibilities as an employer. These rules

SAMPLE 8
PROCESS DOCUMENTATION

PROCESS DOCUMENTATION
BRONWYN BOOKKEEPING INC.

Process Name: Accounts Receivable

Process Goals: To bill clients and collect monies owed in a timely manner. To minimize bad debts and to maximize customer goodwill.

Process Tasks:

- Bill client for services rendered within one business day of work completion.
- Send statements of account to all clients who have outstanding accounts at the end of every calendar month. Statements will be sent by the fifth of the following month.
- Telephone all clients who have accounts outstanding for 45 days to request payment.
- Send final notice statements of account to all clients who have outstanding accounts for 60 days.
- Liaise with the collection agency regarding delinquent accounts.
- Process receipts and update accounting system the day of the receipt.

will be different in every jurisdiction, so make sure your information is correct. Call your local government office or speak with your accountant about it. This will save you considerable grief in the future.

Most jurisdictions have rules on the following employee-related topics:

- ✍ The type of workplace you must provide for an employee
- ✍ The minimum wage you can pay
- ✍ How hazardous materials with which the employee comes into contact must be stored. (Usually the most dangerous material in a bookkeeping practice is correcting fluid!)

✍ How much paid vacation time and how many sick days an employee is entitled to

✍ What deductions you must withhold from an employee's paycheck and remit to the government

✍ How maternity leaves are to be handled by the employer

✍ Under what circumstances you can fire an employee and how much notice an employee needs to be given

There may be dozens of other rules that you must follow, so make sure you understand them before hiring.

Attracting quality employees

Once you have drawn up a job description and familiarized yourself with applicable laws, you're ready to advertise for your first employee. You know what you want the employee to do and you know what skill set you are looking for. But how can you express that in an ad? And how do you make your ad more attractive to potential candidates than those of your competitors?

Your ad will have several components:

(a) *The job description.* Have a clearly worded description so that candidates get a good sense right away of what's involved in the job and whether they have the requisite skills.

(b) *The business description.* Describe your business and its industry.

(c) *The requirements.* Here's where you tell the candidates what they need to have in the way of education, experience, or technical skills. Be as clear as possible so that you do not have to wade through dozens of résumés with unsuitable qualifications.

(d) *Contact information.* Describe how the candidates should respond to the ad: by telephone, fax, e-mail, or in person. Including this information will save you from unwanted interruptions in your business day. It can also help you weed out unsuitable candidates right away. For example, if your ad states that potential candidates should fax their résumés and three people show up in person, this tells you that these three might not be very good at following rules. In some positions this might be a plus, but in most situations this can be a negative quality.

(e) *Tone.* The tone of your ad is difficult to quantify, but it tells potential employees a lot about your business and the workplace environment. If your environment is casual and relaxed, you will want to convey that by using an informal tone in your ad, which will let candidates decide up front whether or not that is the environment they want to work in.

Sample 9 is an actual ad I ran in my accounting practice.

Think of your ad as a way to present your business to highly skilled, motivated potential employees. Remember that your clients will also read your ad. They will get a strong sense of the quality of your staff from what you are asking for in the ad, so make sure your ad exudes professionalism and demands the same from employees.

Once you have a number of résumés in front of you, it's time to select the top candidates. Start by removing any candidate who does not have the background or skills asked for in the ad. (You will almost certainly get some of these, especially in a tough job market.) Have a look at the remaining résumés. Are there candidates who are clearly more qualified than others? Is there someone who claims to have outstanding attention to detail but who misspells several words in the cover letter? Is there someone with important skills that you did not even consider when placing the ad?

Narrow your field to a half-dozen candidates or fewer. You will want to interview several people, as you are also honing your hiring skills. You want to gain as much experience as possible at the task.

Interviewing potential candidates

It's now time to talk to your potential candidates. There are many theories on the interview process, and it would be a good idea to read at least one book on interviewing skills.

The purpose of the interview is for the candidate and the employer to find out enough information to assess whether this would be a good job fit. Never forget that the candidate will be interviewing you too. Ensure that you are prepared and professional — the same qualities you are looking for in an employee.

It's best to have your interview questions prepared ahead of time. That way you'll know you've asked everything you meant to and you will be able to compare answers among candidates.

Create beans, don't just count them!

If you want to be a key team member in a fast-paced, fun, and different kind of accounting firm, then we want to hear from you!

Our new Director of Compliance Services will have the following skills:

- The ability to provide top-notch client service
- Outstanding, proven leadership skills
- Experience in an accounting firm
- Above-average computer skills
- A positive, upbeat attitude

The **REWARDS** are many!

- Above-average compensation
- A dynamic, exciting work environment
- The ability to shape your own career
- A performance-based bonus structure

Please send résumé along with covering letter to:

Mohr & Company
111 Any Street
Anytown, Anystate 98766

Deciding how much to pay an employee is an art.

During the interview, talk to the candidate about your business. Tell them about how you've systematized processes and about your growth plans for the future. An appropriate candidate will be interested in learning more about your business.

Ultimately, you will make your decision based on a combination of factors, including the candidates' answers to your questions, their professional image, their enthusiasm, their salary expectations, and your own "gut feeling." As you become more experienced in human resource management, your instincts will be sharper and more valuable to you.

Employee Compensation

Deciding how much to pay an employee is an art. There are many considerations to keep in mind, including what value the employee is to your company. Every employee contributes to the bottom line in some fashion.

The day you hire your first employee, you are leveraging yourself; that is, you are creating more potential growth than would otherwise be possible. You can determine the value of an employee to the company in much the same way you might assess the value of a capital asset acquisition. You will be paying money out (wages) over time in order to get future revenue streams (the increase in business you will now be able to bring in). You will be getting value from the employee as long as the future inflows are more than the outflows.

Determining market rates

Although it's important for you to analyze the value of an employee to your particular company, a stronger determinant of value is what this person is worth to your competitors. What use is knowing that the new bookkeeper is worth $7 an hour to you when he or she would be able to get $15 an hour from another employer? If you offered $7, the employee either wouldn't take the job or wouldn't stay very long.

Market forces drive wage rates, and you'll have to pay a competitive wage to retain your employees for the long term. How do you know what other employers are paying? Here are some ways to find out:

✍ *Review the want ads in your local paper for a few weeks.* Get a sense of what skills are being asked for. Many of the ads will show the hourly rate being offered.

✍ *Call your local temporary help agency.* They should be able to give you an idea of the going rate for certain skill sets. (They also might try to convince you that you don't need to hire someone on permanently and that a temp would be a better choice.)

✍ *Network with other business owners.* Find out what they pay their staff. Check with the accounting regulatory organization in your jurisdiction to see if they have published wage surveys for the bookkeeping industry in your country.

Having insider knowledge about wage rates will make you more confident that the rate you are offering to employees is competitive (in line with industry standards). You could even tell prospective employees what information your rate is based on.

The importance of benefits

As you go through the process of determining what the market value is of your new employee, look at what benefits are generally offered. Standard benefit packages include the following:

✍ Prescription drugs

✍ Dental

✍ Short-term disability

✍ Long-term disability

✍ Group term life insurance

Benefits are important to most employees, and they will take these into consideration as they decide which position to accept.

Find a good insurance agent that deals with small-business group plans. Go over the costs with the agent and consider offering a benefits package on top of salary. (Make sure you put the cost of the insurance into your monthly budget.)

Sick days are another benefit offered by many employers. This allows employees paid time off when they are sick or have a family emergency. Standards vary, but six sick days per year is usual. You do not have to budget any extra cost into your cash flow for sick days. You will simply pay your employees when they are off sick. The only cost to you is lost productivity.

Performance-based compensation

There was a time when an employer would pay its employees an hourly wage or weekly salary, the employee would work eight hours a day, and that would be it.

The problem with that scenario is that the goals of the employee are not necessarily aligned with the goals of the employer. The employee wants to exchange the required labor for the amount of money the job pays. There is no benefit to the employee of working harder, being more efficient, or coming up with new ways to do things.

On the other hand, the employer's objectives are to make money for the company and grow the business. These conflicting objectives can cause problems for the firm. In the late 1990s, a new compensation model began to emerge, one that pays employees to do the "right things" for the company. It is called variable pay, performance-based pay, or a host of other titles that all mean the same thing.

Paying for value

Performance-based pay is based on the premise that an employee will do what they are compensated to do. A portion of the total compensation package is based upon clear, agreed-to criteria. The employee receives regular performance evaluations and the variable pay component is based on that assessment.

In order for a performance-based compensation system to work, it needs to have the following components:

- ✐ *Clearly defined requirements.* Employees need to know exactly what is expected of them.

- ✐ *Controllable objectives.* Employees must be able to control the criteria upon which they are being evaluated. For example, it would be pointless (and demoralizing) to compensate an employee based on net income if they have no control over net income. On the other hand, if an employee is responsible for the expense budget, it would make sense to compensate her or him partially on control over that budget.

- ✐ *Objectives in line with the overall business plan.* It's important that the variable pay criteria fit within the overall plan of the business.

✍ *Simplicity*. If the criteria are too complicated to remember on a day-to-day basis, the plan will not be remembered by employees as they do their jobs, thereby making it ineffective.

The performance evaluation process

Once the performance criteria have been set, you will need to determine how they are to be measured. The measures should be as objective as possible and easy to understand. For example, if the criteria is "Answers the phone using the company script," the measurement should be percent of overheard telephone calls that were correctly answered.

Many performance evaluation systems use numerical scoring systems. This makes the process easier. A final score in a certain range would mean 100 percent of the variable pay. Lesser scores would mean lesser percentages of the total variable pay. Again, it's critical that the employees understand the process, otherwise it may seem arbitrary and pointless to them.

How often should you evaluate your employees? At a bare minimum, annually. However, it may make sense to do it as often as monthly or quarterly, to keep the job requirements firmly fixed in the employees' minds. This makes it easier for them to incorporate the requirements into their day-to-day performance.

Once the performance evaluation has been completed, meet with your employees one-on-one to go over the evaluation. Allow time for them to give their input into the process as well. This time together should be free of distraction, so consider meeting off-site somewhere or at least in a room with no telephone. Making sure that you will not be disturbed reinforces to your employees that you take this process seriously and, most likely, so will they.

At the end of the evaluation, draw up an action plan with your employee, outlining areas to work on and specific steps the employee will take to improve his or her performance in those areas. Let your employee develop the action plan. Your role here is just to guide and assist. If the employee develops the solutions, there is a much higher probability he or she will implement those solutions.

Keeping tabs on employee performance

The employee evaluation process is ongoing. It's not something to jam into a desk drawer and haul out every three months. It's important

At the end of the evaluation, draw up an action plan with your employee.

to monitor employee performance throughout the evaluation period and make notes with specific dates and times, not only of issues that need to be addressed but also of the great things your employee is doing. Reinforcing positive behavior will pay you dividends.

Another important concept is ongoing feedback. The employee should never be surprised by a performance evaluation. If there are any serious breaches of performance, they should be discussed with the employee immediately and not saved up for the performance evaluation. If there are small things that you feel should be addressed, do it as you go. Give the employee the opportunity to correct problems before the formal performance evaluation.

Sample 10 at the end of this chapter (also on the accompanying CD-ROM) is an employee evaluation form you can customize to your own needs. It was designed for a quarterly performance review.

Firing Employees

One thing no small-business owner wants to think about is firing employees. It's one of the hardest tasks you will ever have to perform as an employer. Not only is it disruptive from an operations standpoint, but it also has implications on personal relationships and finances. How would you feel if you had to fire a single mother and remove her only source of income?

The best way to avoid this is to spend considerable time and effort up front in the hiring process. It's also critical to give feedback in the employee evaluation process so that you are both "on the same page" regarding expectations and obstacles. Sometimes, however, an employment situation just doesn't work out no matter how hard both parties have tired. How do you know it's time to let someone go? Here are some signs:

- Negative client feedback
- Tension with other employees
- A significant reduction in productivity
- Inability to complete job functions without constant supervision and prodding
- Declining morale in the office

Any one of these signs can be due to a number of factors. Only after you have discussed the problems with the employee and have given him or her an opportunity to fix them should you consider termination. You will also have to be familiar with employment law in your jurisdiction so that you do not end up faced with a wrongful termination lawsuit.

There are costs involved in hiring, training, supervising, and firing employees. How you handle these activities can have an impact on your bottom line, so take the time to do it right.

Chapter Summary

- ✌ It's time to consider hiring an employee if the extra revenue you can generate from having your time freed up exceeds the costs of the employee.

- ✌ Have a good grasp of the job processes in your business and what exactly you would have an employee do before you start the hiring process.

- ✌ Compensating employees based on achieving targets that are in line with your business goals ensures that everyone is working toward the common good.

- ✌ Waiting too long to fire a problem employee can be as bad or worse than hiring an employee too fast.

EMPLOYEE EVALUATION FORM

EMPLOYEE EVALUATION FORM

The composite score of this appraisal will determine the bonus level and will be applied as follows:

SCORE	BONUS
0.00–4.99	0%
5.00–5.50	10%
5.51–6.00	20%
6.01–6.50	30%
6.51–7.00	40%
7.01–7.50	50%
7.51–8.00	60%
8.01–8.50	70%
8.51–9.00	80%
9.01–9.50	90%
9.51–10.00	100%

Name of individual being assessed:_____

The following scale will be used for the evaluation:

- 9–10 An exceptional skill. This individual consistently exceeds behavior and skills expectations in this area.

- 7–8 A strength. This individual meets most and exceeds some of the behavior and skills expectations in this area.

- 5–6 Appropriate skill level. This individual meets a majority of the behavior and skills expectations in this area. There is a generally positive perspective toward responsibilities.

- 3–4 Not a strength. This individual meets some behavior and skills expectations in this area, but sometimes falls short.

- 1–2 Least skilled. This individual consistently fails to reach behavior and skills expectations in this area.

- N/A Not applicable or not observed.

WORK PERFORMANCE AND INDIVIDUAL SKILLS

- Gets the job done right the first time   N/A 1 2 3 4 5 6 7 8 9 10
- Completes work in a timely manner   N/A 1 2 3 4 5 6 7 8 9 10
- Completes work accurately   N/A 1 2 3 4 5 6 7 8 9 10
- Effectively works within rules and policies   N/A 1 2 3 4 5 6 7 8 9 10
- Makes timely decisions   N/A 1 2 3 4 5 6 7 8 9 10
- Has good verbal communication skills   N/A 1 2 3 4 5 6 7 8 9 10

- Technical skills are up to date   N/A 1 2 3 4 5 6 7 8 9 10
- Writing is neat and legible   N/A 1 2 3 4 5 6 7 8 9 10
- Work is organized and complete   N/A 1 2 3 4 5 6 7 8 9 10
- Recognizes problems and identifies underlying causes   N/A 1 2 3 4 5 6 7 8 9 10
- Has good strategic skills   N/A 1 2 3 4 5 6 7 8 9 10
- Is persistent in reaching goals   N/A 1 2 3 4 5 6 7 8 9 10
- Is effective at working within time limits   N/A 1 2 3 4 5 6 7 8 9 10
- Knows how to prioritize work   N/A 1 2 3 4 5 6 7 8 9 10
- Develops effective systems and improves processes   N/A 1 2 3 4 5 6 7 8 9 10
- Keeps a clean, organized work area   N/A 1 2 3 4 5 6 7 8 9 10
- Brings expertise to the job   N/A 1 2 3 4 5 6 7 8 9 10
- Keeps knowledge up to date by reading, researching, etc.   N/A 1 2 3 4 5 6 7 8 9 10
- Coaches, motivates, and helps develop others   N/A 1 2 3 4 5 6 7 8 9 10
- Is trustworthy, open, and honest   N/A 1 2 3 4 5 6 7 8 9 10
- Is prompt and on time   N/A 1 2 3 4 5 6 7 8 9 10
- Has a positive outlook   N/A 1 2 3 4 5 6 7 8 9 10

Total points for this section_____

CLIENT SERVICES

- Treats clients like business partners   N/A 1 2 3 4 5 6 7 8 9 10
- Identifies, understands, and responds to appropriate needs of clients   N/A 1 2 3 4 5 6 7 8 9 10
- Presents ideas clearly and simply   N/A 1 2 3 4 5 6 7 8 9 10
- Listens attentively to clients   N/A 1 2 3 4 5 6 7 8 9 10
- Solicits and provides effective feedback   N/A 1 2 3 4 5 6 7 8 9 10
- Uses the company phone protocol   N/A 1 2 3 4 5 6 7 8 9 10
- Provides awesome service — goes that extra mile to do things right   N/A 1 2 3 4 5 6 7 8 9 10
- Is friendly and courteous to clients   N/A 1 2 3 4 5 6 7 8 9 10
- Knows clients' businesses   N/A 1 2 3 4 5 6 7 8 9 10
- Replies promptly to client requests   N/A 1 2 3 4 5 6 7 8 9 10
- Looks after clients in a timely manner   N/A 1 2 3 4 5 6 7 8 9 10
- Develops systems for better client services   N/A 1 2 3 4 5 6 7 8 9 10

- Keeps others informed about client needs   N/A 1 2 3 4 5 6 7 8 9 10
- Balances client requests with business
  requirements   N/A 1 2 3 4 5 6 7 8 9 10

Total points for this section_____

TEAMWORK

- Supports the team's goals   N/A 1 2 3 4 5 6 7 8 9 10
- Puts the interests of the team before
  self-interest   N/A 1 2 3 4 5 6 7 8 9 10
- Builds consensus and shares relevant
  information   N/A 1 2 3 4 5 6 7 8 9 10
- Treats others fairly   N/A 1 2 3 4 5 6 7 8 9 10
- Takes responsibility for own actions   N/A 1 2 3 4 5 6 7 8 9 10
- Does his or her part to get things done   N/A 1 2 3 4 5 6 7 8 9 10

Total points for this section_____

MANAGEMENT AND LEADERSHIP SKILLS

- Manages resources effectively   N/A 1 2 3 4 5 6 7 8 9 10
- Takes initiative to make things happen   N/A 1 2 3 4 5 6 7 8 9 10
- Takes informed, calculated risks   N/A 1 2 3 4 5 6 7 8 9 10
- Makes well-reasoned, timely decisions   N/A 1 2 3 4 5 6 7 8 9 10
- Follows through to deliver results   N/A 1 2 3 4 5 6 7 8 9 10
- Communicates and sets clear expectations   N/A 1 2 3 4 5 6 7 8 9 10
- Anticipates and prepares for change   N/A 1 2 3 4 5 6 7 8 9 10
- Has people skills — is fair, honest,
  dependable, and approachable   N/A 1 2 3 4 5 6 7 8 9 10
- Provides supportive and guiding
  leadership — does not try to control   N/A 1 2 3 4 5 6 7 8 9 10
- Delegates duties skillfully   N/A 1 2 3 4 5 6 7 8 9 10
- Organizes and prioritizes work   N/A 1 2 3 4 5 6 7 8 9 10
- Is visionary — sees the big picture   N/A 1 2 3 4 5 6 7 8 9 10
- Applies fairness to any action   N/A 1 2 3 4 5 6 7 8 9 10
- Coaches and develops team   N/A 1 2 3 4 5 6 7 8 9 10

Total points for this section_____

BUSINESS DEVELOPMENT

- Actively seeks new clients   N/A   1   2   3   4   5   6   7   8   9   10
- Maintains required networks   N/A   1   2   3   4   5   6   7   8   9   10
- Provides input to business development
  strategy   N/A   1   2   3   4   5   6   7   8   9   10
- Suggests new services to provide to clients   N/A   1   2   3   4   5   6   7   8   9   10
- Learns new skills to assist in company
  growth   N/A   1   2   3   4   5   6   7   8   9   10

Total points for this section_____

INNOVATION

- Constantly benchmarks "best practices"   N/A   1   2   3   4   5   6   7   8   9   10
- Performs frequent process reviews   N/A   1   2   3   4   5   6   7   8   9   10
- Solicits process-improvement feedback   N/A   1   2   3   4   5   6   7   8   9   10
- Suggests new goals for team growth   N/A   1   2   3   4   5   6   7   8   9   10
- Researches better ways to do things   N/A   1   2   3   4   5   6   7   8   9   10
- Creates systems and procedures to
  make jobs easier   N/A   1   2   3   4   5   6   7   8   9   10
- Presents strategic ideas in order to
  improve organization and service   N/A   1   2   3   4   5   6   7   8   9   10

Total points for this section_____

SCORING

Total questions answered ÷ Total points from all sections = Average score

_____ ÷ _____ = _____

Bonus level achieved_____

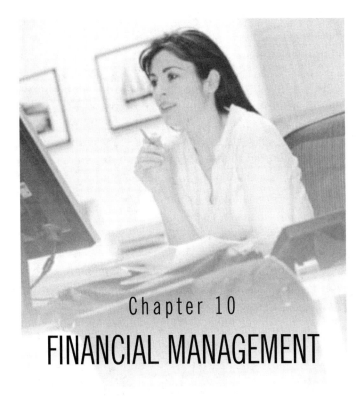

Chapter 10
FINANCIAL MANAGEMENT

Every business needs to prepare at least a basic budget to project revenue and expenses for the next 12 months. A budget is your road map that guides your business on the path to financial success.

Budgeting 101

Preparing a budget — especially your first — can seem like a daunting prospect. You will, over time, develop this skill and will be able to project your company's revenue and expenses effectively. Let's take a look at projecting your revenue first.

Projecting revenue

Revenue can be the most difficult budget item to predict, especially when you are first starting your bookkeeping practice and have no historical financial information to work from. You can assume that your monthly revenue will show a steep incline. (If you have one client in the first month and two in the second, your revenue will increase by 100 percent.)

It makes sense to work backwards from your marketing plan. For example, if you plan to network with ten business associates per month, you might estimate that every month, you may garner six new clients from that source. You will then estimate what you think the average monthly billing for each of those clients might be and build your revenue projections from there. As you improve your ability to bring new work in the door, you can adjust your projections accordingly.

Projecting expenses

To project your expenses, start by listing all of your known expenses. You will have certain expenses that never fluctuate, such as equipment lease payments and office rent. You will also have expenses that vary, either in step with sales levels or because of other factors. Some examples of variable expenses are office supplies and postage.

Start by mapping those expenses you know for certain. If you are locked into a three-year office lease, you know exactly what your payments will be for the next year. Then start filling in the other expenses. You will need to think about each one as you estimate it. For example, if you know that you will be sending out 5,000 flyers in May, make sure the projected cost is in your advertising budget figure for May. If you are projecting a 20 percent increase in sales, you will probably want to increase your office supplies budget somewhat.

Your wage costs deserve special attention. Make sure you are including all of the costs of the employees, not just the net checks paid to them. Depending on the regulatory environment you operate in, you would also have employee-related expenses such as pension premiums, employment insurance premiums, or health care premiums. These are all costs of having employees and should be included as a projected expense. Also, if you are projecting a big jump in sales, make sure you can achieve it with the employees you have. If not, make sure you include the wage costs of new employees in your plan.

Included as Worksheet 6 (and as an Excel template on the accompanying CD-ROM) is a budgeted income statement you can amend to your particular situation. You should keep your budget up to date and always be looking 12 months into the future. At the end of every month, you will assess how your actual numbers compared to your budget assumptions, then drop that month off the budget and add another month on to the end.

BUDGETED INCOME STATEMENT

Company Name: _____

Month →											Total
Account											
REVENUE											
EXPENSES											
Cost of goods sold											
Advertising											
Bank charges											
Office expenses											
Professional fees											
Rent											
Supplies											
Telephone & utilities											
Vehicle expenses											
Wages											
TOTAL EXPENSES											
NET INCOME											

Fixed and Variable Costs

In order to fine-tune your budget, it's important to understand how costs behave. All of a company's expenses can be categorized by their behavior, that is to say, whether they vary with the level of a company's revenue or not. The two basic categories of expenses are fixed and variable. All of the expenses on your company's income statement are one of these two types.

Fixed expenses

Fixed expenses are a company's expenses that are independent of the sales volume. Even if you do not bill out a single dollar, you will still incur these costs. A few examples of fixed expenses are rent, utilities, and office wages. You still need a place to run your business out of, electricity for lights, and someone answering the phones, whether you sell anything or not.

It's important to note that fixed expenses are only fixed in the short run. Eventually, at higher sales volumes, you will need a larger warehouse, more power for the equipment, and more office staff. However, for the time being, we will only look at the range of sales volume in which the fixed expenses remain constant.

Variable expenses

Variable expenses, as their name suggests, vary directly with the sales revenue of the company. The most common examples of variable costs are cost of goods sold (in the case of a retailer) and cost of goods produced (in the case of a manufacturer). For a bookkeeping practice, your only cost of sales generally would be the amount you pay staff members to provide client services.

For example, if you pay your employees (assuming they only work the number of hours needed) $14 per hour for work that you bill out at $25 per hour, you can see how the expense would stay in lockstep with your revenue. As revenue rises, so would this expense.

Why Is Cost Behavior Important to My Business?

You need to know how your costs behave because, armed with that information, you can analyze your income statement and plan for business growth. Two critical concepts are related to cost behavior analysis: break even and capacity.

Fixed expenses are a company's expenses that are independent of the sales volume.

Break-even point

Your company's break-even point is the point where your revenue is sufficient to cover your expenses. Your first thought might be that this would happen at zero sales, but remember, you still have fixed costs to cover whether you bill out anything or not.

Take the following example:

Revenue per hour billed	$25
Cost per hour billed	17
Gross margin (GM)	8

So, for every hour you bill out your employee (and yourself, on the assumption that you are paying yourself the same rate), you net $8. Now, what if your annual fixed expenses looked like this?

Rent	$7,500
Utilities	1,250
Office supplies	595
Total fixed expenses	9,345

How many hours would you have to bill per year to cover your fixed expenses? To calculate your break-even point, the formula is —

Total fixed expenses ÷ Gross margin ($) =
Annual hours billable (to break even)

In the foregoing example, the calculation would be as follows:

$9,345 ÷ $8 = 1,168 hours

You would therefore need to bill out 1,168 hours between yourself and your employee to keep the doors open. If you bill more, you will make a profit. If you bill less, you will lose money.

Instead of number of hours, you can also look at break even by calculating the total billings you need to break even. Using the above example, we would start by calculating a gross margin (GM) percent.

GM per unit ÷ Revenue per unit = GM%

Continuing with the same example, the calculation would be:

$8 ÷ $25 x 100 = 32%

You could then determine your break-even sales using the following formula:

$$\text{Overhead} \div \text{GM\%} = \text{Break-even sales (\$)}$$

$$\$9,345 \div .32 = \$29,203$$

You would therefore need to have annual revenue of $29,203 to be able to keep the doors open.

Most small businesses never take the time to calculate their break-even point. Most feel that revenue will be whatever it is and they can't do anything about it. You can see from the above example why it would be important to know how much your sales have to be to stay in business.

Capacity

Another critical concept is that of capacity. Not only is it important to know how much you need to have in billings to keep the doors open, you need to know how much it is possible to bill out with your current cost structure. If you're a manufacturer, your plant and equipment will only physically handle so many units before you need to move to larger premises and purchase new equipment. If you're in a service business, eventually, at higher revenue levels, you will need to hire more staff and have larger offices. In a bookkeeping practice, there are only so many hours between yourself and any other staff that you can bill out. You can think of your break even as the minimum you need to do and capacity as the most you can do.

Let's look at an example:

Number of hours in a work year (per person)	1,950
Average number of hours spent on admin. activities	250
Number of hours available to charge to clients	1,700
Average billing rate	$25

Capacity is calculated by using the following formula:

$$\text{Billable hours} \times \text{Billing rate} = \text{Maximum revenue (\$)}$$

$$1,700 \times \$25 = \$42,500$$

In this example, each of your full-time bookkeepers should be able to charge out 1,700 times $25 annually to clients. This tells us that if you are alone in the practice, the maximum revenue you can generate is $42,500. So it would be ridiculous to budget for $75,000 in billings without planning for a new staff member.

Basic Ratio Analysis

The subject of ratios is one that makes most small-business owners' heads hurt (even bookkeepers')! Financial analysts and stockbrokers regularly assess the ratios of large, publicly traded companies, but many small businesses do not even consider ratios when they prepare their financial information. Why should you care about ratios?

Ratios are a useful tool for you to compare your business activities year over year.

- *Lenders care about them*. Your bank will certainly care about monitoring ratios. They want to see how you're doing in comparison to other businesses they are lending to and in comparison to the standards they have set for lending.

- *They help you spot trouble*. Ratios are excellent indicators of financial health. Much like a high blood pressure or high cholesterol reading at the doctor's would signal impending trouble, out of kilter ratios do the same for your company.

- *They chart history*. Ratios are a useful tool for you to compare your business activities year over year. For example, is your working capital ratio steadily improving or not? (This and other ratios are discussed later in this section.)

- *They allow comparisons*. Ratios are a useful tool for you to compare your business activities to those of other companies. Without using ratios, it can be difficult to compare companies of different sizes.

Ratios can be grouped into different categories based on the type of information they provide. The basic categories of ratios are solvency or liquidity ratios, asset and debt management ratios, and profitability ratios.

Solvency or liquidity ratios

Solvency ratios (sometimes called liquidity ratios) indicate how well your business can pay its bills in the short term without straining cash flows. As you can well imagine, your lenders are usually quite interested in the short-term solvency of your business (they want to make sure they get their money back!), and these are commonly calculated ratios. They include the current ratio and the total debt ratio.

Current ratio

This ratio is one of the best measures of whether you have enough resources to pay your bills in the next 12 months. The current ratio is calculated as:

Current assets ÷ Current liabilities = Current ratio

The current ratio can be expressed in either dollar figures or times covered. For example, a company has total current assets of $4,325 and current liabilities of $3,912. (If you need a quick refresher on current assets and current liabilities, please refer to the first book in the *Numbers 101 for Small Business* series, entitled *Bookkeepers' Boot Camp*.) The company's current ratio would be:

$4,325 ÷ $3,912 = 1.11:1

You can say that for every dollar in current liabilities, there is $1.11 in current assets. You could also say that the company has its current liabilities covered 1.11 times over.

To a lender, the higher the ratio the better. Their investment in your company is more secure. The same is generally true for you as the business manager; you want to see the ratio at least 1 or more. However, if your current ratio is abnormally high, it may indicate that you are not using your resources effectively. Here are some reasons why this might happen:

- ✐ Abnormally high work-in-progress levels

- ✐ Surplus cash sitting in a bank account that should be invested long term (or used to pay down current liabilities)

- ✐ An accounts receivable collection problem

Total debt ratio

The total debt ratio measures the long-term solvency of your company. It shows you how highly your company is leveraged, or in debt. The total debt ratio is calculated as:

Total debt ÷ Total assets = Total debt ratio

Just like the current ratio, you can express the total debt ratio in dollars or times. For example, if a company had total debt of $12,673 and total assets of $9,412, its total debt ratio would be:

$12,673 ÷ $9,412 = 1.35:1

In the case of the total debt ratio, you want to see the result 1 or less. The lower the ratio, the less total debt the company has in comparison with its asset base. In the above example, you could express the ratio a few different ways. You could say that for every dollar in assets, the company has $1.35 in liabilities. You could also say that the company is leveraged 135 percent or that its assets cover its liabilities 0.74 times over ($9,412 ÷ $12,673).

As a bookkeeping practice, your debt levels most likely aren't as high as they might be if you were a retailer or manufacturer, but it's a good idea to keep track of this ratio nonetheless.

Asset and debt management ratios

Asset and debt management ratios tell you how well your company is managing its resources to generate sales. These ratios consist of work-in-progress (WIP) turnover, receivables turnover, and times interest earned.

Work-in-progress (WIP) turnover

The work-in-progress turnover ratio answers the question: How long do I let my client work build up before I bill it? This is an important question because increasingly stagnating WIP can have a serious impact on your cash flow. The WIP turnover rate is calculated as follows:

Billed hours ÷ work-in-progress = WIP turnover rate

If your total billed hours for the past 12 months were 1,526 and your unbilled WIP hours were 72, the WIP turnover ratio would be:

1,526 ÷ 72 = 21.2 times

We could say that you can turn over our billings 21.2 times in a year. A more useful interpretation is to calculate days' billings in WIP, which is:

365 days ÷ WIP turnover days' billings

In this example, the calculation would be:

365 ÷ 21.2 = 17.2 days

This tells us that, on average, the work-in-progress sits for just over 17 days before it is billed. Some companies calculate the average WIP for the year (beginning WIP plus ending WIP divided by two), and some companies use the ending WIP. It all depends on what you want to track. Using average WIP gives you a historical perspective, that is, what happened during the year, whereas using the ending WIP gives you a forward look at your current WIP levels.

In general, you would want this ratio to be as low as possible. If the days in WIP start creeping up, it may be a sign that you're not billing work out as regularly as before.

Receivables turnover

While the WIP turnover ratio tells you how fast you bill your services, the receivables turnover ratio tells you how fast you generally get the money for the billings into your bank account. The receivables turnover ratio is calculated much like the WIP turnover ratio:

Revenues ÷ Accounts receivable = Receivables turnover

If your revenues were $113,423 and your receivables balance was $18,903, the ratio would be calculated as:

$113,423 ÷ $18,903 = 6.0 times

You can also look at the average number of days before collection:

365 days ÷ Receivables turnover = Days' sales in receivables

In this example, the calculation would be:

365 ÷ 6.0 = 60.8 days

This tells you that, on average, you collect your receivables in just over 60 days. If your credit terms are net 30, this indicates a problem. You would need to examine your credit and collection policies to find out why you don't get your money in 30 days.

Times interest earned

The times interest earned calculation tells you how able you are to meet the interest obligations to your creditors. It is calculated using the following formula:

Earnings before interest and taxes (EBIT) ÷ Interest expense = Times interest earned

If your EBIT was $23,496 and your interest expense was $2,674, then the calculation is:

$23,496 ÷ $2,674 = 8.8 times

This means you could have paid your interest expense almost nine times over. In general, the higher the ratio, the "safer" the company is. It is critical to note, though, that this ratio only looks at the interest portion of creditor obligations, not the required principal repayments. The principal repayments are part of the current ratio (for principal repayments due in the next 12 months) and the total debt ratio (for all principal repayments).

Profitability ratios

The last major category of ratios is profitability ratios. These measure how effectively you are able to use your resources to produce profit. We will look at two ratios in this category: profit margin and return on investment (ROI).

The return on investment tells you what level of return you are getting from the personal money you have invested in your business.

Profit margin

The profitability margin known as the profit margin is a common measure of how well you can translate gross revenue into bottom-line profit. It is calculated as:

Net income ÷ Revenue = Profit margin (%)

If your net income is $22,475 and your revenue is $113, 423, your profit margin is calculated as follows:

$22,475 ÷ $113,423 x 100 = 19.8%

This tells you that for every dollar of revenue, you are generating almost 20 cents in net profit. As you can well imagine, in general, the higher the profit margin, the better off the company is.

Return on investment (ROI)

The return on investment (ROI) ratio is one of the least calculated and most important ratios for small businesses. It tells you what level of return you are getting from the personal money you have invested in your business.

For example, let's say that when you started up the company, you took $7,500 from your savings account and used that money for start-up expenses. You could have taken that same money and invested it in a bond (where it would earn interest income) or in real estate (where it would earn rental income) or one of a hundred other investments. But you chose to invest in your own small business instead. Shouldn't you be making a return on that investment? Absolutely!

Return on investment is calculated using this formula:

Normalized net income ÷ Money invested x 100 = ROI (%)

What do I mean by "normalized" net income? We want to calculate net income as if you are being properly compensated for the hours you work in the business. This is your "employee" or "manager" role. How do you know what you're worth? Start by calculating how much you would have to pay someone else to step into your shoes as the manager of the company. For example, if you would have to pay a replacement $47,000 and you are only paying yourself $25,000 in order to reduce cash flow, then you would subtract the difference ($22,000) from income to get to normalized net income. Here's the calculation for return on investment using the figures provided.

($22,475 – $22,000) ÷ $7,500 x 100 = 6.3%

This means that you are making a 6.3% return on your investment in the company. Probably better than a savings account but not enough to compensate you for the risk of investing in a small business. On top of that, you're getting paid $25,000 for a $47,000 job. You have a ball and chain around your foot because you can never leave your business. No one in their right mind would take over your business and make that kind of money. Not a very cheery outlook!

Ratios are an important tool to help to decipher the story of your business's financial statements.

Key Performance Indicators

One way to track how well you are doing the important things in your business is by defining and tracking your Critical Success Factors, or CSFs. Critical Success Factors are defined as those activities a business undertakes that allow it to succeed.

CSFs are more than just the numbers on your financial statements. Some CSFs relate to measures of quality, customer satisfaction, and how efficiently you are using your resources.

However, before you can do any analysis of your company's Critical Success Factors, you need to examine your business strategy.

Take a few moments to answer the following questions:

1. My business is better than my competitors' because:

   _____

   _____

2. My clients always say that they like it when:

   _____

   _____

3. My clients always say that they don't like it when:

   _____

   _____

4. If I stopped _____,
   my clients would start going elsewhere.

Note that two of the four questions relate to your clients' perception of your company, not your impressions of what they think. It's an important distinction, for your clients may have a very different view of you and your business than you think. How do you know what your clients think? Ask them! Set up a procedure where they are asked to fill out a feedback form when they experience your service. (See Sample 7 on page 106 for a customer satisfaction form you can adapt to your purposes.) Ask clients what they like and don't like. Ask why they might choose to do business elsewhere. Ask what you are doing well and what you could be doing better. You may be surprised by the results.

The answers to the four questions above give you a list of those activities you need to make sure your business is doing regularly and consistently. Review your list. You will most likely find that the items on it relate more to your clients' perceived value in your service, not just its cost. Companies that compete only on cost will always suffer in the long run, for there will always be someone else who can do the work for less. (This idea is discussed further in chapter 3, on pricing your services.)

Now that you have defined your Critical Success Factors, you need to be able to make sure you are on track. How do you measure them, especially when some are nonfinancial?

Have staff members fill out a standard form when client complaints occur, outlining both the problem and its resolution.

The measurements of Critical Success Factors are called Key Performance Indicators, or KPIs. To recap the jargon, Critical Success Factors are things your company must do to thrive, and Key Performance Indicators are how those things are measured.

Here is a typical list of Critical Success Factors:

✍ *Personal service* — making sure the client gets to speak with a staff member when the work is done

✍ *Quality* — making sure the service is accurate and on time

✍ *Quick problem resolution* — making sure all client complaints are handled quickly and in a manner that impresses the client

✍ *Fast turnaround* — making sure that the client meets all filing and other deadlines and that the work has been done in the time promised

All four of these CSFs can be measured, even though some of them are nonfinancial. Some examples of the Key Performance Indicators that would track whether you are on target with your CSFs are:

✍ *Personal service*. Provide every client with a feedback form when he or she purchases your product or service. One of the questions should be, "Was a staff member available to answer all of your questions?" Your KPI then becomes how many "Nos" are reported on the surveys.

✍ *Quality*. Track how many client complaints are received. Have a target number. Any number above that is unacceptable.

✍ *Quick problem resolution*. Have staff members fill out a standard form when client complaints occur, outlining both the problem and its resolution. Have a staff member follow up with a telephone call to the client seven days after the incident to ask if the client is happy with the resolution. The measures could be the satisfaction rating of the client and the number of days between the initial complaint and the client's satisfaction.

✍ *Quick turnaround*. Track the average number of days that work stays in the office before completion.

These are some of the ways that nonfinancial indicators can be measured and tracked. Once the measures have been determined, it's important to set your expectations to measure against.

What happens if your Key Performance Indicators start to slide? You've been tracking your Key Performance Indicators for months, and this month, several of the indicators seem to show problems. What do you do?

When this happens (as it inevitably will), you need to discover the source of the problem. A business could face many problems that would impact its Key Performance Indicators, including employee illness, cash flow crunch, breakdown in processes, and inattentiveness to client needs. If the problem is short term, such as employee illness, there is no need to take drastic action. However, you will want to see if there is a way to make your operations less vulnerable to the illness of a single employee.

If the problem seems to be in the underlying processes, it's time to put new procedures in place to make sure the Critical Success Factor is being met. Have there been changes in the external business environment? New competitors in the industry? Quality control problems with the work being done? These are all situations that require rethinking and reformulation of your business plan. If you can see the icebergs, you will have a much better chance of being able to steer around them.

Receivables Management

We talked about monitoring receivable ratios earlier in the chapter to ensure that your average collection period mirrors your credit terms. It's important to watch for changes in your average collection period because this can act as an early warning indicator of problems. For example, if your terms of sale are net 30 and your average collection period has traditionally hovered around 29 days, that suggests that your credit and collection policies are working. If, however, the average collection period starts to climb to 40 days or 50 days, this indicates that customers are taking longer to pay and you will need to reexamine your credit and collection policies.

Another way to look at your receivables is through an aging schedule. This is a listing of your accounts receivable by vendor. The receivables are sorted into aging "buckets," usually current, 30 days, 60 days, and 90 days. The percentage of receivables in each bucket is calculated. If your percentages of overdue receivables start to go up, this also indicates a problem that needs addressing. Here is an example of an aged accounts receivable report:

Small Company Inc. Aged Accounts Receivables February 29, 20--					
Client	Current	30 days	60 days	90 days	Total
Baxter Box Co.	47.34	182.89	612.49	19.49	862.21
Brandywine Inc.		1,712.56			1,712.56
Drawton Inc.	1,983.67				1,983.67
Merna Finlayson	197.58				197.58
Jim Fox	563.12		49.97		613.09
J. Morgan				798.37	798.37
Total	2,791.71	1,895.45	662.46	817.86	6,167.48
Percentage	45	31	11	13	100

Notice that 31 percent of the receivables are 30–59 days old, 11 percent are 60–89 days old, and 13 percent are 90 days or older. This tells us that 55 percent of the total receivables are overdue. If that total shot up to 65 percent, for instance, you would examine the cause as to why your customers were paying more slowly. You would adjust your policies or enforce your existing policies as needed. Even with no change in the percentages, this table still reveals a problem with collections that should be investigated.

Payables Management

You probably don't think of your suppliers as financing your operations, but if you are receiving credit terms from them, it is simply another form of lending that has a cost attached to it.

The suppliers that offer credit terms will either offer a discount for early payment or interest on overdue accounts (or both). How do you know when it's to your benefit to take advantage of these terms?

Let's look at the example of a supplier that offers the terms 2/10 net 30. This means that if you pay the bill in 10 days, you will get a 2 percent discount. In any event, the bill is due in 30 days. Taking advantage of this credit is free to you for ten days. You will either pay in ten days to take the maximum advantage of the free credit or you will pay in 30 days to get the longest possible use of cash in exchange for giving up the discount. Paying the extra 2 percent essentially buys you an extra 20 days of credit.

Now let's look at the cost of not taking the discount. If the order was for $1,000, you would have had the opportunity to only pay $980 if you had taken the discount ($1,000 x .98). Essentially, by not taking the discount, you are borrowing $980 for an extra 20 days and you are paying $20 for that privilege ($1,000 – $980). The effective annual rate is calculated as follows (a two-step process):

$$\$20 \div \$980 \text{ x } 100 = 2.04\%$$

There are 18.25 20-day periods in the year (365 ÷ 20). The effective annual rate is calculated as:

$$(1.0204)^{18.25} - 1 = 44.6\%$$

This means that you are essentially making 44.6 percent on your money by paying 20 days early. That's a pretty good return! If your company is cash-flow poor, you must weigh the strategy of stretching out your payables against the cost of doing so. In the above situation, it would be more beneficial to maintain a line of credit with the bank in order to take advantage of early payment discounts.

On the other end of the spectrum, many suppliers charge interest on overdue accounts. A common term of sale is 2 percent per month for each month overdue. What is the true cost of taking advantage of this form of financing? At first glance, it would appear to be 24 percent annually (2% x 12 months), but it is actually higher than that, due to the negative pull of compounding. The effective annual rate is actually as follows:

$$(1 + 0.02)^{12} = 26.82\% \text{ annually}$$

It would therefore cost you 26.82 percent to use this source of financing past 30 days. That is higher than bank financing and even higher than credit card financing. You must weigh this cost against the short-term cash-flow benefit of using this source of financing.

Another consideration in not paying within the credit window is your relationship with your suppliers. They are not in the business of lending money, and the only purpose of charging you interest is to encourage you to pay your bill. They would rather have you pay on time than pay them interest. If you repeatedly pay later than the due date, you may strain your relationship with that supplier.

The general conclusion of this discussion is that you should pay your payables within the credit terms offered and take advantage of discounts if your cash flow allows. In order to keep track of discount and penalty dates, it's important to have an adequate payables tracking system, which is discussed in the next section.

Tracking due dates

In order to be able to take advantage of supplier discounts and avoid supplier interest charges and penalties, you need to set up an effective payables tracking system. Most accounting software, like MYOB and QuickBooks, can be set up to monitor those critical dates and produce a warning report of upcoming deadlines.

One thing to make sure you know is how a supplier determines the discount date. For example, if your supplier offers a 2 percent discount for payment in 10 days, do they count the days to the date your check is dated, the date the envelope is postmarked, or the date it's received? This is important information. I've seen many small businesses in my accounting practice that do not track this well and think they are getting the discount when, in fact, they are not. They mail out the payment on day 10 and it doesn't get credited to their account for another few days after that. Adequate tracking systems will help you to know if you're getting the discount or not.

What to do if you fall behind

Hitting the cash-flow wall is something no one wants to think about, and good up-front planning will ensure you never have to. However, even solid businesses sometimes run into unexpected cash-flow problems. In this type of situation, it's critical to restrict the outflows of cash and speed up the inflows. How do you decide what to pay first and what to put off?

Earlier in the chapter, we talked about the cost of credit. There are several ways to order your payables to decide which ones to pay first and which ones to defer.

    ✍ *Compare the credit costs.* One way to determine which payables to pay first is to look at the comparative costs of the credit. You would pay first the ones that cost the most to maintain.

    ✍ *Consider your suppliers.* Look at which suppliers you least want to annoy. These would be the suppliers that you want to maintain an ongoing relationship with and that you will need to order from in the future. One example is your landlord if you rent your work premises. Chronic lateness in paying your rent will probably make him or her less inclined to perform repairs and maintenance for you.

✍ *Consider the consequences.* Look at the potential consequences of nonpayment to each supplier. For example, if you get behind on remitting your payroll taxes to the government, they have the ability to freeze your business bank account. This would effectively halt your operations and cause grave damage to the company.

It's always a good idea to discuss your situation with your suppliers. Some will be more sympathetic than others, but none will be sympathetic if you just avoid them completely. Give them some general time frames for probable payment, but don't commit yourself to a payment plan you can't maintain. You may wish to provide them with postdated checks as a show of good faith, but make sure you have the money to cover them. The only thing worse than a customer that pays late is a customer that pays late and bounces checks!

Chapter Summary

- ✌ Tracking the ongoing financial results of your business is critical to its success.

- ✌ Understanding cost behavior will help you to make better budget predictions.

- ✌ Your Key Performance Indicators measure your company's critical processes.

- ✌ Monitoring your receivables and payables can improve your cash flows immensely.

Chapter 11

GROWING YOUR BUSINESS

This chapter takes a preliminary look at growing your business. I introduce the three ways to grow your business, how to track your progress, and what to do when things aren't working. For a more in-depth review of business growth strategies, you may wish to refer to *Managing Business Growth* (Self-Counsel Press, 2005).

Many small businesses use the splatter approach to marketing and growth. They throw together some advertisements for the paper or perhaps for radio. They prepare some flashy brochures and mail them to all the potential clients in town. They take out a big ad in the business pages of the telephone book. Then they cross their fingers and hope that business floods in the door.

There are several reasons why this approach doesn't work. For starters, it's far more expensive to attract new clients than it is to keep current ones. (We first looked at this concept in chapter 8, on marketing and promotion). And until you improve the way new clients are handled in your business, you may simply have more people deciding *not* to buy from you.

Smart companies focus on the clients they already have.

Let's take a look at the different ways you can grow your business.

The Three Methods of Business Growth

There are only three ways to grow your business. Any growth strategy you can think of falls into one of these three categories: attract new clients, sell more to your current clients, or sell to your clients more often.

(a) *Attract new clients.* This is the obvious one. Get new people in the door to buy your product or service. This is the type of strategy that advertising supports.

(b) *Sell more to clients.* Another way to grow your business is to sell more to your current clients. This is a key strategy of companies like McDonald's ("Would you like fries with that?") and Amazon.com ("If you liked that, you will love this"). Your current clients already know you and like what you have to offer. Chances are, they will like more of what you have to offer. This strategy is also known as upselling.

(c) *Sell to clients more often.* The second strategy focused on selling clients more every time they buy from you. This strategy focuses on having them buy from you more often.

You can see that these three methods encompass all business growth strategies imaginable. However, many small-business owners concentrate only on the first strategy, getting new clients. This can be dangerous for a number of reasons.

    ✍ *Marketing costs money.* As mentioned earlier in this chapter, it is expensive to market to new clients. This is where the advertising budget goes.

    ✍ *Loyalty takes time.* New clients are not yet loyal to you. It takes time to build relationships with clients.

    ✍ *New clients don't know you.* It's hard to market to a cold audience. You are trying to peddle your wares to people who do not know you or your business practices. It is a leap of faith on their part to buy from you.

Smart companies focus on the clients they already have. These are the clients who have purchased from you before, know what you have to offer, and like it. They know you, your business practices, and your premises. Buying from you is comfortable and familiar to them. Why not ensure that you are getting the most from these customers?

Let's look at some strategies to bolster your business using your existing client base.

The Concept of Leverage

The great thing about understanding the numbers behind your business growth strategy is that it gives you power that you wouldn't otherwise have. Making even small incremental changes in each of the three growth areas provides you with leverage. This means that the numerical result of all of the changes is greater than the sum of the individual pieces. Let's look at an example.

Say your business currently has 1,000 clients. On average, each client spends $175 each time they use your services. Your clients use your services on average twice annually. What is your current revenue? The formula looks like this:

> No. of clients x Average transaction x Average no. of transactions per client = Annual revenue

Using the numbers in the example, the calculation would be as follows:

> 1,000 x $175 x 2 = $350,000

What would happen if you put strategies in place to make small changes in the number of clients, the average amount of each sale, and the number of times your clients use your services?

Perhaps you're aiming for only a 5 percent increase in your client base, a 10 percent increase in the amount of the average transaction, and you want to provide services to clients three times a year instead of two. What's the impact on your bottom line?

> Client base: 1,000 + 5% = 1,050

> Average transaction: $175 + 10% = $192.50

> Average no. of transactions per year: 2 + 50% = 3

Your new annual revenue, using the formula already described, would be:

> 1,050 x $192.50 x 3 = $606,375

That's a 73 percent increase in bottom line revenue from small changes in each of the three areas of business growth. You haven't doubled your client base. You haven't doubled your prices. You've simply made small, incremental changes in each area that add up to a leveraged result.

Tracking Your Business Growth

Now let's look at some strategies to implement and track these three growth areas.

How to attract new clients

How much did your client base grow last year? If you're like many small-business owners, you really have no idea. Only when you start tracking your statistics do you get a grip on what happens when there are changes in your asset base.

Take some time to track how many active clients you have right now. If you're using an accounting program such as QuickBooks or Simply Accounting, you'll be able to go into the client list and count your clients. If you're on a manual system, you may have to go back through your invoices for the last year and make a list.

Chapter 4, in reference to client management, discussed assessing the quality of your clients on a scale of A to D. As your client list grows, continue to rate your clients on a regular basis. Remember that A is for clients who buy lots from you, pay promptly, bring in other new clients, and are pleasant to deal with. These are clients you love doing business with. D clients are those who are price-sensitive, complain often, and pay late or not at all. B and C are somewhere in between. This ranking gives you an idea of what types of clients you want to attract. Clearly, you only want to attract new A clients.

Strangely enough, you may find that most of your advertising is targeting D clients. Every time you advertise that you have the lowest price, you attract price-sensitive clients. The problem with these types of clients is that you will never instill loyalty in them. The minute a competitor can come up with a lower price (and someone will always be able to do that), these clients are gone.

Now, take some time to analyze how you are going to attract new A clients. Because a bookkeeping practice is a business where trust

Take some time to analyze how you are going to attract new clients.

is important, you most likely get most of your new clients from referrals from your existing clients. Why not send a letter to your existing A clients and offer them a 10 percent discount on their next order if they bring in a referral? "Oh, no," you say. "I can't afford to do that!" Let's look at the numbers using the example from above:

Existing client — average invoice	$175.00
10% discount	(17.50)
New customer — average annual billing	$350.00
Lost revenue	17.50
Gained revenue	350.00
Net gain	$332.50

If you want to be even more detailed, you would also count the cost of the stamp and paper for the letter. You would even get more mileage out of this strategy if you implement the other business growth methods and increase the average value of each sale and the number of annual visits per client.

Ways to sell more to clients

The next strategy is to increase the average value of every transaction, the business growth method also known as upselling. The key is to make sure your clients are aware of all the products and services you have to offer. When a client comes into your practice for monthly bookkeeping, ask if they need a quarterly financial statement review. Make saying yes easy for them. Give them choices instead of expecting them to pipe up if they want something. They might not even be thinking about buying anything except what they came for unless you remind them of your additional services.

Another method of keeping your products and services fixed in the minds of your clients is by keeping in touch on a regular basis. Send them mailings or newsletters at least quarterly. Give them valuable information while reminding them that you are ready and waiting to handle their business.

Sell to clients more often

You've now got more clients coming in the door and they're buying more when they come. Now we want to have them come in more often. Accomplishing this will be different in every industry. In the restaurant industry, for example, a business owner can send out coupons to current customers to entice them to eat more often at their restaurant rather than at another. In the auto repair business, the owner can put together a package for customers to have a lube, oil, and filter change for a set price. In your bookkeeping practice, entice your clients to come to see you monthly rather than quarterly, or quarterly rather than annually.

Growing your business without tracking your results is like running a marathon without looking at the clock. It doesn't give you any indication of how you're doing and whether you're achieving your goals.

Growth benchmarks should be a part of your monthly operating plan (see chapter 12), and you should track new clients, average revenue per client, and average number of client visits. As well, you should track where your new clients are coming from. Are they visiting your business because of an advertisement you ran? Or has someone referred them to you? Knowing this helps drive your growth efforts in the future.

A template for tracking business growth can be found on the accompanying CD-ROM.

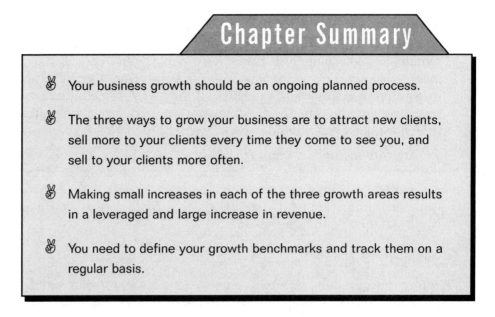

Chapter Summary

- Your business growth should be an ongoing planned process.

- The three ways to grow your business are to attract new clients, sell more to your clients every time they come to see you, and sell to your clients more often.

- Making small increases in each of the three growth areas results in a leveraged and large increase in revenue.

- You need to define your growth benchmarks and track them on a regular basis.

Chapter 12

PLANNING FOR SUCCESS

So far in this book, we've looked at the major aspects of planning and controlling your bookkeeping business, from developing new clients to managing work flow to tracking financial results. Now we need to take a step back and look at the planning and control process as a whole. Our goal is to set up a system to collect, monitor, and report on the critical information that you need to run your bookkeeping business smoothly and profitably. Let's start by taking a look at the planning cycle.

The Planning Cycle

How do you go about planning your business? How often do you need to track and record financial benchmarks? And then, what do you do with that information?

A business's planning cycle looks like this:

PLAN → CONTROL → GROW → FINE-TUNE → PLAN

Note that planning comes first in the cycle. There is no point trying to control what you do not plan for. As I mentioned in the book's introduction, the survival rate of small businesses is low. More than 80 percent of small businesses in North America fail in the first five years, and 80 percent of the rest fail within the next five years. Many of these businesses have failed to plan their operations from the beginning. When you think about all of the time, energy, and money you have invested in starting up your business, doesn't it make sense to take time to chart a path first?

Step 1: Make a plan

Every business needs to start with a plan. When I use the word "plan" here, I'm not simply referring to that document your banker insisted you prepare from a template when you first started up your business. I'm referring to a real business plan: a living, breathing document that changes and grows with your business, a document that guides your business through the icebergs and into safer seas. A typical business plan will include the following ingredients:

- ✍ Projected revenue and expenses for at least a 12-month period
- ✍ Projected cash-flow statement
- ✍ Target ratios
- ✍ Break-even and capacity calculations
- ✍ A capital replacement budget
- ✍ A list of critical success factors and their related key performance indicators
- ✍ An employee compensation and evaluation strategy
- ✍ A promotion strategy with timelines

There are many ways to put together this information. Once you have determined what information you need, you must decide how often you need it. Some information, such as accounts receivable data, employee productivity numbers, and sales statistics, you may need weekly. Other information, such as a full budget analysis, cash-flow statements, and details on product returns, you may need only monthly. And, of course, at the end of the fiscal year, you will need the full package of financial information.

Step 2: Get control

The next step in the planning process is controlling the actual performance of the business. There are as many ways to collect and control the information as there are ways to plan. Every business will tailor the information flows to its unique needs. What follows is one method of preparing weekly updates and a monthly management operating plan.

The weekly flash report

Some of your financial information needs to be available to you quickly and easily. Every week you will want to view this information so that you have an early warning if your business is starting to derail. It's much easier to make alterations to a ship's course when it has only been off-course for a week than it is after a month. What information do you need to see weekly? That's up to you. Here are some common weekly statistics for a small business:

- Weekly sales
- Average number of days in receivables
- Employee productivity
- Aged receivables
- Aged payables
- Working capital ratio

Once you have determined what information you need to see weekly, set up a system so that the data can be gathered as quickly and as automatically as possible. If you have office staff, teach them how to gather the information. As the manager, your goal is to only have to view the information and make plans based on it. Of course, if you are a one-person business, you will not have this luxury and will have to pull together the information yourself. Try to avoid getting so bogged down in the gathering that you don't have time to analyze the data.

Ultimately, your weekly flash report should boil down to a one-page-at-a-glance summary of whether or not you are on target. If you have weekly team meetings, this is good information to present so that everyone is aware of the larger picture. Get one of your staff to present the weekly flash report at a team meeting. This gives your team a more in-depth understanding of the planning process and the business itself.

Sample 11 is an example of a weekly flash report.

WEEKLY FLASH REPORT

GARDEN CITY BOOKKEEPING SERVICE
WEEKLY FLASH REPORT

Week of: July 11 to 17, 20--

		Actual	**Target**	**Variance**
1.	Revenue	$2,013	$2,200	**$187 unfavorable**
2.	Aged receivables balance	$14,682	$15,000	**$318 favorable**
3.	Average days in receivables	27	30	**3 favorable**
4.	Overall billable hours	37	35	**2 favorable**
5.	New clients	1	2	**1 unfavorable**

NOTES:

- Two jobs did not come in this week as planned; will be in next week's sales
- Follow-up calls to clients with balances over 40 days resulted in a 90% collection rate
- Newspaper ad resulted in fewer responses this week than expected and only one new client. Need to look at changing ad copy.

The monthly management operating plan

You will also want to see the bulk of your management information on a monthly basis. The typical monthly management operating plan includes the following items:

- ✐ A monthly budget showing actual versus planned revenue and expenses
- ✐ A monthly cash-flow statement showing actual versus planned inflows and outflows of funds

- ✍ Ratio analyses including turnover and capital ratios

- ✍ An analysis of all actual key performance indicators compared to the plan

- ✍ A synopsis of the external and internal business environment and how it has affected the business

- ✍ A thorough analysis of employee productivity

- ✍ A summary of promotional efforts and their measurable impact on results

Again, it's important to involve your staff in the assessment process. They may have insights and explanations that you would not see.

Sample 12 shows how you might want to set up your monthly management meetings.

The performance highlights would show the key indicators that are the most relevant to your business for planning purposes. Sample 13 provides a template for performance highlights.

The management discussion and analysis portion of the monthly meeting delves into the operating climate that your business faced in the past month. It talks about things such as opportunities, challenges, and successes. Sample 14 provides a template for the management discussion and analysis.

Step 3: Focus on growth

Only after you have a good handle on your business's operations should you focus on growth. Many small businesses are so concerned right from the start about growing that they do not know what impact the growth is having on their business. If you do not have a plan, new clients can suck your business dry, absorbing more resources than they are adding revenue. Growth must be profitable and sustainable. For a more detailed discussion on business growth, you may wish to refer to the book *Managing Business Growth* (Self-Counsel Press, 2005).

Step 4: Fine-tune your business

Now that you have set the course for your business, focused on its goal, and tracked its progress, it's time to make some minor adjustments to the path it is on. Once you have several months or years of data to work with, operational patterns will emerge. For example,

SAMPLE 12
MONTHLY PLANNING MEETING NOTES

MONTHLY PLANNING MEETING NOTES

Date of meeting:

Time:

Those in attendance:

	Agenda item	Presented by	Action items	Deadline	Responsibility
1.	Review of last meeting's action items				
2.	Performance highlights				
3.	Management discussion and analysis				
4.	Climate analysis				
5.	Client feedback				
6.	Other business				

you may find that every year, there is a major dip in revenue in August. This seasonality may not have been apparent from the outset. If it is something that you expect will continue, you can alter your plan to reflect that reality. You can also focus your promotional activities to produce benefits during that slow time.

By this time, you will also have a track record of measuring and monitoring the impact of changes on your business. For example, you may have discovered that a 10 percent increase in your print advertising budget will result in a 12 percent increase in sales, or

SAMPLE 13
PERFORMANCE HIGHLIGHTS

PERFORMANCE HIGHLIGHTS

Month ended:_____

		Current Year	Previous Year	% Change
1.	Revenue			
2.	Net income			
3.	New customers			
4.	Billable hours			
5.	Current ratio			
6.	Wages as a % of revenue			

that a tax season "bonus services" promotion results in 15 new tax clients, or that buying a new laptop will increase productivity by 15 percent. You will be able to precisely target your efforts with the skill of a surgeon rather than that of a lumberjack.

Fine-tuning is an ongoing process that involves measurement, comparison, and adjustment. It is a continual refinement of the machine that is your business. Ultimately, your goal is to one day have the machine run without you. That's why you are spending time developing self-diagnostic tools and gauges.

Step 5: Plan some more

Notice that we end up back at the planning stage, thus completing the cycle. Once your company has progressed through an entire business cycle, it's time to plan again. It's a continual process of bettering your business.

The planning and control processes are what set apart outstanding businesses from ordinary ones. Plan properly and watch your business flourish!

MANAGEMENT DISCUSSION AND ANALYSIS

MANAGEMENT DISCUSSION AND ANALYSIS

Month ended:_____

1.	What we did exceptionally well this month:
2.	What we missed our target on:
3.	What changed in our operating environment:
4.	Our main focuses in the coming month:
5.	What indicators will alert us to problems:
6.	Other unexpected or unanticipated events this month:

Chapter Summary

✌ Every business needs a plan: a living, breathing document that changes and grows with your business.

✌ An important part of the plan is the collecting and controlling of financial information on a regular basis.

✌ Involve your staff in the collecting and presenting of financial information for two reasons: to help them understand the financial transactions of the business and to help you gain a more in-depth understanding of your employees' role in day-to-day operations.

✌ The planning process includes fine-tuning the plan to zero in on those benchmarks that are critical to the success of your business.

GLOSSARY

Accounts payable: The amounts owed by a business to its suppliers or vendors for goods and services purchased on credit. Also called trade payables.

Accounts receivable: The amounts owed to a business from its customers or clients for goods or services provided on credit.

Accrual accounting: A method of accounting where income and expenses are recorded in the periods in which they occur, not necessarily the periods in which cash is exchanged.

Accrued liabilities: These are amounts owed by a business to its suppliers or employees that relate to the current period but for which it has not yet been invoiced. Also called accrued expenses.

Bad debts: The estimated amount of credit sales that have become questionable as to collectibility in the current period.

Balance sheet: One of the three main financial statements prepared by a business. The balance sheet displays everything that is owned and owed by the company that has a measurable financial value.

Bank reconciliation: The process of comparing and reporting differences between the bank balance on the bank statement and the bank balance in the ledger.

Book value: The value of assets, liabilities, and equity recorded on the balance sheet of a business. Book value may differ (sometimes substantially) from replacement cost or market value.

Break-even point: The point in a business's operations where revenue is sufficient to cover expenses.

Budgeting: The process of planning and projecting revenue, expenses, and capital expenditures for future fiscal periods.

Capacity: The upper limit of a company's ability to produce a product or service.

Capital assets: The tangible operating assets of a business. These assets generally provide the business with operating capacity as opposed to being held for resale. They have a relatively long life.

Cash basis accounting: A method of accounting in which financial transactions are recognized in the period in which cash is transfered, not necessarily the period to which the event relates. Generally accepted accounting principles usually do not allow cash basis accounting.

Cash-flow: The inflows to and outflows from an entity, regardless of the source.

Cash-flow statement: Also known as the statement of changes in financial position, this is one of the three main financial statements of a business. In its most general terms, it shows why there is an increase or decrease in cash during the year. These increases and decreases are summarized into operating, financing, and investing activities.

Certified general accountant (CGA): A professional accounting designation in Canada that requires candidates to meet certain standards before being granted the designation.

Certified management accountant (CMA): A professional accounting designation widely recognized in the United States and Canada. CMAs must pass rigorous standards before attaining the designation; however, the focus of training is more on internal management practices as opposed to public accounting.

Certified public accountant (CPA): A widely recognized professional accounting designation in the United States. To be a CPA, one must meet educational and experience requirements, as well as pass a uniform examination to qualify for a state license to practice.

Chartered accountant (CA): A widely recognized professional accounting designation in Canada, the UK, and Australia. A CA must meet educational and experience requirements and pass a uniform examination to be able to hold a public accounting license. Requirements vary between the countries, as the designation is administered by different professional regulatory bodies.

Chart of accounts: The set of accounts used by a business that make up its general ledger. These accounts are standard to that particular organization, and all transactions must be recorded using these standard accounts unless a change is granted by management.

Competitive intelligence: The process of finding who your competitors are and what they are doing to maintain a competitive advantage in the marketplace.

Compound interest: Interest earned on your interest. You earn compound interest when you leave your interest in an investment so that during the next period, you earn interest on both your principal and the reinvested interest.

Controller (comptroller): The "big cheese" accountant in an organization. The controller oversees all accounting functions and sometimes operates as the company's chief financial officer.

Cooking the books: A term for the process of making the financial results look good. Although there are many acceptable choices that can be made with respect to accounting policies, some of which will make the books look better, "cooking the books" generally involves fraudulent methods of recording nonexistent transactions or transactions with values different from what is being recorded.

Cost accounting: An older term for management accounting. Cost accounting is usually more narrowly defined as accounting for the costs of manufacturing goods and apportioning them to the correct products in the correct periods.

Cost-based pricing: Pricing of services based on costs of inputs, which involves calculating how much it costs you to provide a service, then building in a profit margin. Also called cost-plus pricing.

Cost of goods sold (COGS): The purchase or manufacturing costs of the goods that were sold during a particular period. The costs related to the goods not yet sold are accounted for in inventory on the balance sheet.

Creditor: A person or other entity that has loaned money or extended credit to a business.

Current assets: A category of assets on the balance sheet that represents cash and assets that are expected to be converted into cash within one year.

Current liabilities: A category of liabilities on the balance sheet that represents financial obligations that are expected to be settled within one year.

Current ratio: A solvency ratio that measures whether a business has enough resources to pay its bills in the next 12 months. Calculated by dividing current assets by current liabilities.

Debits and credits: Accounting terminology representing the increases and decreases in ledger accounts. Debits represent increases to assets and expenses, and decreases to liabilities, revenue, and equity accounts. Credits represent increases to liabilities, revenue, and equity accounts, and decreases to assets and expenses.

Debt: The amounts owed by a business to outside persons or businesses. It is sometimes more narrowly defined as to exclude accounts payable and only include loans that have fixed interest rates and repayment schedules.

Dividends: The portion of earnings (either current or retained from prior periods) that have been distributed to the shareholders in the current operating period.

Double-entry bookkeeping: The method of bookkeeping first documented in 1494 that recognizes that each financial transaction affects at least two balances simultaneously.

Earnings: A term usually used interchangeably with net income (that is, revenue less expenses).

Entrepreneur: A person who envisions and creates a business. This person may or may not be either an investor or manager in the ongoing operations.

Exit strategy: A plan for a company's owners to either sell or wind up the business.

Financial statements: The main summary financial reports produced by a business's accounting and bookkeeping system. The three main financial statements are the balance sheet, the income statement, and the cash-flow statement.

Financing activities: One of the three main summary categories on the cash-flow statement. Financing activities are those transactions between a business and its sources of funding. They include the borrowing and repayment of debt, the issue and retraction of share capital, and the payment of dividends.

Fixed assets: An older term for capital assets.

Generally accepted accounting principles (GAAP): The collection of standards and practices required to be used by businesses to record and present the results of their financial activities and their records of what they own and what they owe. GAAP can be different between industries and between countries.

Goodwill: In the general sense, goodwill represents the intangible asset that a business possesses by virtue of its good name in the community, strong and loyal customer or client list, and brand-name recognition. In its more narrowly defined accounting sense, goodwill represents the intangible value that has been paid for when a company purchases another company. This is the only type of goodwill that generates accounting recognition. It is carried as an asset on the balance sheet.

Gross income: Another term for revenue.

Gross margin: Represents revenue minus the cost of goods sold in the period.

Income statement: One of the three major financial statements of a business. (The balance sheet and the cash-flow statement are the other two.) The income statement shows operating activity over an operating period from revenue, expenses, and extraordinary gains and losses.

Insolvent: A term used to describe a business that does not have enough assets to meet its debt obligations in the short term. Insolvency must be corrected quickly or it could lead to bankruptcy.

Internal control: The procedures set up in a business to prevent errors and fraudulent activity.

Inventory: Goods held for resale but not yet sold at the end of an operating period. In a manufacturing environment, inventory would include goods in the process of being made, finished goods, and raw materials. In certain service industries, it would include time spent on customer activities but not yet billed out.

Investing activities: One of the three main summary categories on the cash-flow statement. Investing activities include the purchase and sale of capital assets, including land, buildings, equipment, and furniture and fixtures.

Key performance indicators: Numeric measures of the factors that are critical to the success of a business.

Liability: Something that is owed by the business to outside parties. Liabilities can be current or long-term, depending on when the obligation is to be settled.

Liquidity: The ability of an asset to convert into cash or its ability to be easily sold. Assets are shown on the balance sheet in the order of their liquidity, the most liquid (cash) being first.

Long-term liability: An obligation that is not expected to be settled within one year. The current portion of these liabilities (i.e., present value of payments due within one year) is shown in the current liability section of the balance sheet.

Management accounting: The accounting done internally to assist managers in their decision-making role. Management accounting generally encompasses budgeting, forecasting, unit costing, and ratio analysis.

Mortgage payable: The balance of a business's debt that is secured by the business's real property. The most common reason for the borrowing is the purchase of a land and building in which the business will operate. The present value of the mortgage payments due within one year are presented as current liabilities on the balance sheet, and the present value of the payments due more than one year out are presented in the long-term liability section.

MYOB: A popular accounting software program for small businesses.

Net book value: The difference between the original cost of a capital asset and its accumulated depreciation.

Net income: The income left in an accounting period after all expenses have been deducted from revenue. The term net income is only used if the revenue exceeds the expenses.

Net loss: The deficit for an accounting period that occurs when the expenses for that period exceed the revenue.

Obsolescence: Generally used in reference to inventory, obsolescense is the loss in use of an item due to new and improved items taking its place, changes in customer preference, or other conditions unrelated to the physical condition of the item.

Operating activities: Those activities in which a business engages that create its main source of profit.

Operating cycle: The period of time it takes for a business to complete a full round of its operating activity. It is the time it takes to convert cash back into cash, which includes buying inventory, selling inventory, and collecting the receivables.

Owners' equity: The amounts owed by a business to its owners rather than outside parties.

Partnership: One of the three main forms of business ownership. A partnership is an unincorporated business with two or more owners. Partnerships are jointly owned by the partners and do not have a separate "legal life" of their own.

Performance-based pay: An employee compensation model in which a variable pay component is based on clearly defined requirements and regular employee assessment. Also called variable pay.

Periodic inventory: A method of accounting for inventory by which all purchases throughout the operating cycle are posted to cost of goods sold. Inventory is physically counted at the end of the period, and the adjustment for goods sold is made at that point. With this method, inventory is correct only at the end of the period.

Perpetual inventory: A method of accounting for inventory by which goods are recorded as being removed from inventory as they are sold. With this method, inventory is always theoretically correct and is checked against a physical count at the end of the period.

Posting: The process of summarizing general journal entries and recording them in the general ledger.

Profit: See *Net income*.

Profit and loss (P&L) statement: Another name for an income statement.

QuickBooks: A popular accounting software program for small businesses.

Retained earnings: The amount of cumulative net income that remains in the business that has not been paid out to the owners.

Revenue: The amount of net assets generated by a business as a result of its operations.

Shareholder: An owner or internal investor of a corporation.

Simply Accounting: A popular accounting software program for small businesses.

Sole proprietorship: One of the three main forms of business ownership. A sole proprietorship is an unincorporated company that is owned by a single owner. It has no "legal life" of its own.

Solvency: The ability of a company to settle its liabilities with its assets.

Statement of cash flows: One of the three main financial statements. The statement of cash flows explains the changes in assets, liabilities, and net equity for the period.

Statement of changes in financial position: An older term for the statement of cash flows.

Taxable income: The amount of net income that is subject to income tax. It will differ from net income per the financial statements by any differences between GAAP and tax regulations.

Total debt ratio: A measure of the long-term solvency of your company. Calculated by dividing total debt by total assets.

Transaction: A financial business event that is recorded in a business's books.

Turnover time: The amount of time it takes a business to get new work in the door, process it, and return it to the client.

Upselling: The business growth strategy that entails selling existing customers more products or services.

Working papers: A set of documents prepared for the external accountants to verify the balances and calculations made in a business's books.

Write-down: An accounting entry to reduce the carrying value of an asset, such as inventory, to its market value.

Write off: A slang term for expensing a cost in the books of a business.

The following Worksheets and Resources are included on the CD-ROM for use on a Windows-based PC. The documents are in MS Word and/or Excel format, as well as in PDF.

Worksheets

- Business Plan
- Budgeted Income Statement
- Cash-Flow Projection
- Client Sign-In Sheet
- Client Survey
- Client Termination Letter
- Employee Evaluation Form
- Evaluating Accounting Software
- Exit Strategy
- Home-Office Expenses
- Management Discussion
- Monthly Planning Meeting Notes
- New Client Checklist
- Performance Highlights
- Process Documentation
- Skills Assessment
- Tracking Business Growth
- Vehicle Expenses
- Weekly Flash Report
- Work In Sheet

Resources

- Online Resources
- Recommended Books

OTHER BOOKS BY ANGIE MOHR

Numbers 101 for Small Business is a series of easy-to-understand guides for small-business owners, covering such topics as bookkeeping, analyzing and tracking financial information, starting a business, and growing a business. Using real-life examples, Angie Mohr teaches small-business owners how to beat the odds and turn their ideas into successful, growing companies. Mohr is the managing director of Mohr & Company Chartered Accountants and Business Consultants.

BOOKKEEPERS' BOOT CAMP: GET A GRIP ON ACCOUNTING BASICS

ISBN: 1-55180-449-2
$14.95 US / $19.95 CDN

Bookkeepers' Boot Camp teaches you how to sort through the masses of information and paperwork, how to record what is important for your business, and how to grow your business for success!

This book will show you the essentials of record keeping for a small business and why it's necessary to track information. The book will give you a greater understanding of the process of record keeping and a deeper understanding of your business and how it works.

- Manage paper flow
- Understand the balance sheet
- Learn the basics of income statements and cash-flow statements
- Record the sales cycle
- Learn how to account for inventory
- Monitor your budget and cash flow
- Understand transactions between the company and its owners

FINANCIAL MANAGEMENT 101: GET A GRIP ON YOUR BUSINESS NUMBERS

ISBN: 1-55180-448-4
$14.95 US / $19.95 CDN

This book covers business planning, from understanding financial statements to budgeting for advertising. Angie Mohr's easy-to-understand approach to small-business planning and management ensures that the money coming in is always greater than the money going out!

Financial Management 101 is an in-depth guide on business planning. It's a kick-start course for new entrepreneurs and a wake-up call for small-business owners.

FINANCING YOUR BUSINESS: GET A GRIP ON FINDING THE MONEY

ISBN: 1-55180-583-9
$14.95 US / $19.95 CDN

Financing Your Business will show you, in an easy-to-understand manner, how to raise capital for your small business. Whether you are just starting a new business you want to expand an existing business, this book help you to acquire the funds you will need.

Angie Mohr leads you step by step through the process and explores all the options available so that you can devise a financial plan that is suited to your company and goals.

MANAGING BUSINESS GROWTH: GET A GRIP ON THE NUMBERS THAT COUNT

ISBN: 1-55180-581-2
$14.95 US / $19.95 CDN

Managing Business Growth is the third book in the *Numbers 101 for Small Business* series from Angie Mohr. Mohr teaches small business owners how to profitably expend their businesses by using sound financial planning. The book shows you how to measure the effectiveness of your operations, human resources, and marketing to correct inefficiencies, pinpoint new opportunities, and maximize profits.

Many small business owners are successful at what they do, but aren't able to make the next step in expanding their operations without breaking the bank. This book shows how to create a step-by-step financial plan designed to cultivate growth and profits.

Self-Counsel Press